Principles & Practices in English Pronunciation

Principles & Practices in English Pronunciation

Seo Young Yoon & Chung Hyun Lee

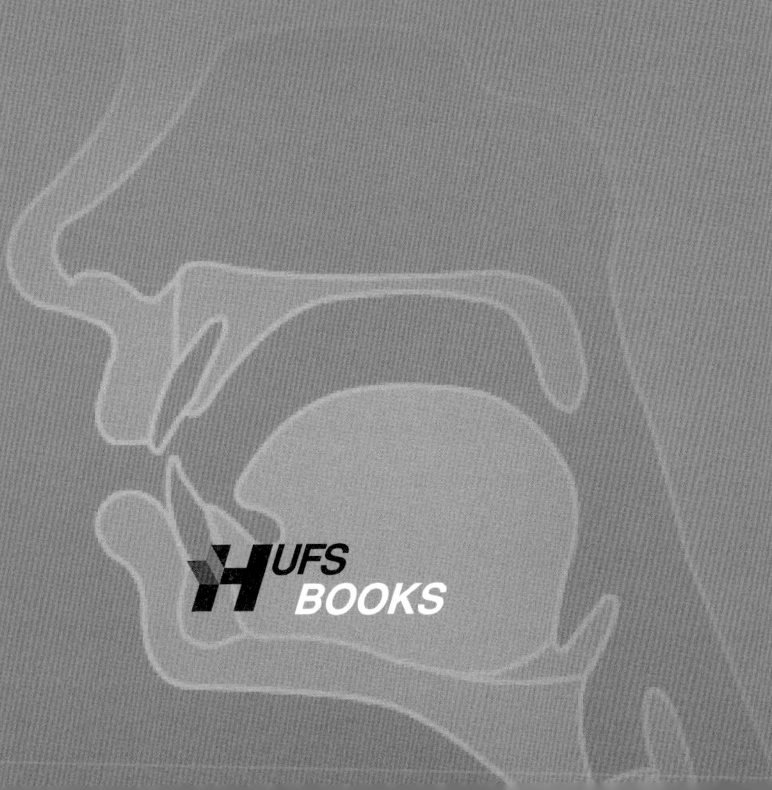

HUFS BOOKS

Principles & Practices in English Pronunciation

First printed August 20, 2011
First published August 30, 2011
The writers Seo Young Yoon & Chung Hyun Lee
The publisher Park, Chul
Hankuk University of Foreign Studies Press Center
270 Imun-dong Dongdaemun-gu, Seoul, 130-791
Tel : 82-2-2173-2495, 2496
Fax : 82-2-2173-3363
Homepage : http://press.hufs.ac.kr
e-mail : press@hufs.ac.kr
Registration of publisher : 6-6 (Apr. 30, 1969)

ISBN 978-89-7464-683-7 18740 ₩16,000 (mp3 included)

Acknowledgement

Many people have supported and encourage the production of this book.

We would like to thank the hundreds of students who helped us in collecting the data required for the research, which this book is based on. Their questions, comments and suggestions along the way were invaluable, and without them, this book would not exist.

We are grateful to the Multimedia Education Center at Hankuk University of Foreign Studies for the immense support for this book. In addition, we would like to thank the staff of HUFS Press Center for the hard work they put in for the publication of this book.

Introduction

1. Aims and Objectives

The current trend in English education in Korea at all levels focus on communicative competence under the banner of globalization. In this respect, the producing comprehensible spoken language, in other words, being understood in the way that was meant to be understood, began to be considered more important than in previous era. Pronunciation is one of the most important basic subskills needed in order to be able to communicate intelligibly in English. It serves as the foundation for building confidence in communication, leading to increased fluency in speaking. For effective learning and using of comprehensible pronunciation to happen, both segmental and suprasegmental need to be addressed. Moreover, communicable environment in which the learners can experience the language through social interaction and collaboration needs to be provided.

Therefore, the goals and objectives of the book is to enable learners to understand and be understood in communicative situations they may face using English, to build learner confidence so that they may enter these communicative situations with ease, and to enable learners to monitor their speech to make further adjustments and improvements based on objective standards. In order to achieve the goals and objectives, the students will be trained to improve their English pronunciation in terms of both production and perception.

2. Course Components

This book consists of 4 main sections. The first section consists of 5 units on the introduction and suprasegmentals of spoken English. It is followed by 10 units on consonants and 6 units on vowels of English. The consonants and vowels addressed in this book focus on those that were found to be problematic for Korean learners. 16 units on the general patterns of spoken English are provided to be studies simultaneous and accumulatively along with the segmental sections of consonants and vowels.

The book is accompanied by an audio CD with mp3 files. It contains recordings of all examples, texts, and dialogues. It is intended both for classroom use and independent work. The materials are recorded in American accent by native speakers of American English. The students are to use it as guidance for practice and for giving peer feedback.

3. Note to teachers

For maximized effect, allow students to use voice recording and bulletin board system where they can upload their samples, give peer feedback, and receive peer and teacher feedback. Online resources provided in the appendix should be incorporated to provide additional exposure and practice. For detailed description, refer to unit i introduction to English Pronunciation-Approaches in Learning and teaching the English Sound system.

Teachers can choose the course component according to the students' proficiency level and needs, but a suggested syllabus for a 16 week syllabus is provided as follows.

Proposed Syllabus

Weeks	Units
Week 1	Unit 1 Introduction to English Pronunciation
Assignment	Pre-Diagnostic Test
Week 2	Unit 2 The Sound System of English
Assignment	Stresses in English Tend to Recur
Week 3	Unit 3 Intonation Unit 22 Letters, Numbers, Dates & Addresses Unit 23 Descriptive & Set Phrases
Assignment	Giving Personal Information
Week 4	Unit 4 Word Connection Unit 5 Reduction Unit 24 Meaningful Utterances Unit 25 Filler Utterances
Assignment	Dialogues
Week 5	Unit 6 Introduction to Consonants Unit 7 Consonants T & D Unit 26 Thought Groups
Assignment	Introducing Yourself
Week 6	Unit 8 Consonant L Unit 27 Emphasis Unit 28 Added Details
Assignment	A Walk in the Park
Week 7	Unit 9 Consonant R Unit 29 Contrasting and Showing Alternatives
Assignment	Little Red Riding Hood
Week 8	Midterm Exam

Weeks	Units
Week 9	Unit 10 Consonant TH Unit 30 Question Intonation Unit 31 Tag Question Intonation
Assignment	The Speech Accent Archive
Week 10	Unit 11 Consonants F & V Unit 12 Consonants P & B Unit 32 Listening Well
Assignment	Weather Forecast
Week 11	Unit 13 Consonants S & Z Unit 14 Consonants /ʃ/ & /ʒ/ Unit 33 Continuing a Story
Assignment	Gettysburg Address
Week 12	Unit 15 Other Consonants M, N , NG, H, K & G Unit 16 Introduction to Vowels Unit 17 Vowel Schwa
Assignment	Self Written Text
Week 13	Unit 18 Vowel /æ/ Unit 34 Quoting Others Unit 35 Humor
Assignment	News Report
Week 14	Unit 19 Vowel /ä/ Unit 36 Depending on the Context
Assignment	JFK Inaugural Address
Week 15	Unit 20 Vowels /ɪ/ & /i/ Unit 21 Vowels /u/ & /ʊ/ Unit 37 Polite Alternatives
Assignment	Personal Opinion
Week 16	Final Exam

Table of Contents

Review for Consonants

Vowels

Review for Vowels

General Patterns of Spoken English

Table of Contents

List of Tables

List of Figures

List of Figures

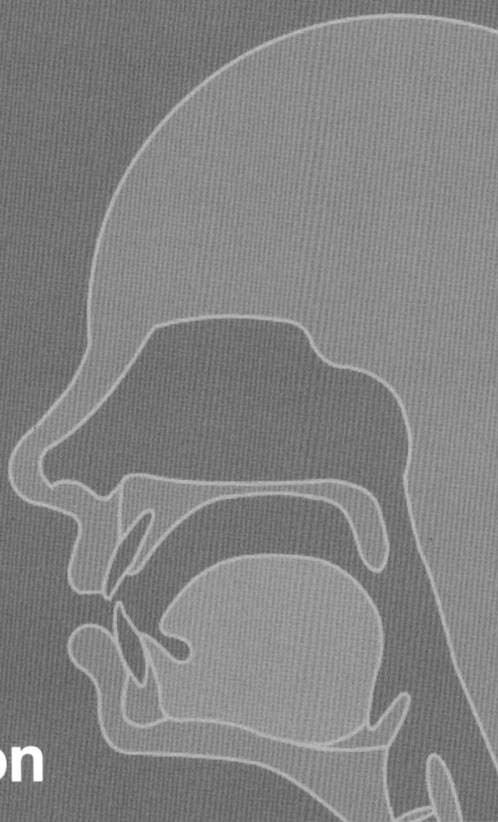

Introduction

Unit 1

Introduction to English Pronunciation

Speech Chain & Speech Organs

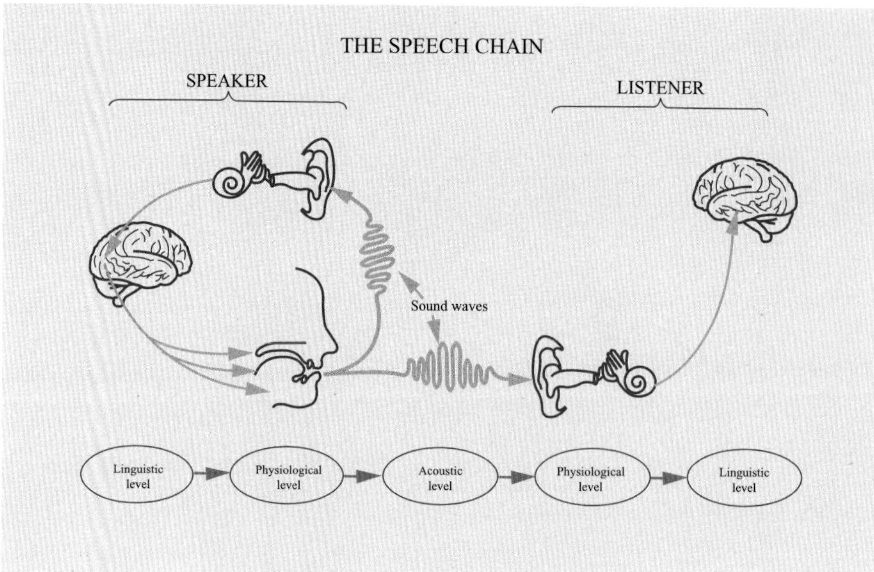

Figure 1. Speech Chain (Denes & Pinson, 1963)

There are three ways in which pronunciation can be approached. One is articulatory phonetics. It deals with the production of speech. Another area is called acoustic phonetics which is about the transmission of speech itself. The third is called auditory phonetics. It addresses how sounds are received by the listener. This book will mostly deal with articulatory phonetics along with auditory phonetics since the ability to produced sounds and the ability to recognize sounds are both important in successfully carrying out comprehensible and intelligent conversation.

Speech Organs

In order to produce sounds, the speech organs need to be used appropriately. There are three major categories of speech organs.

- Respiratory organs: lung, and respiratory tract
- Phonatory organs: larynx
- Articulatory organs: vocal tract, nasal cavity, and oral cavity

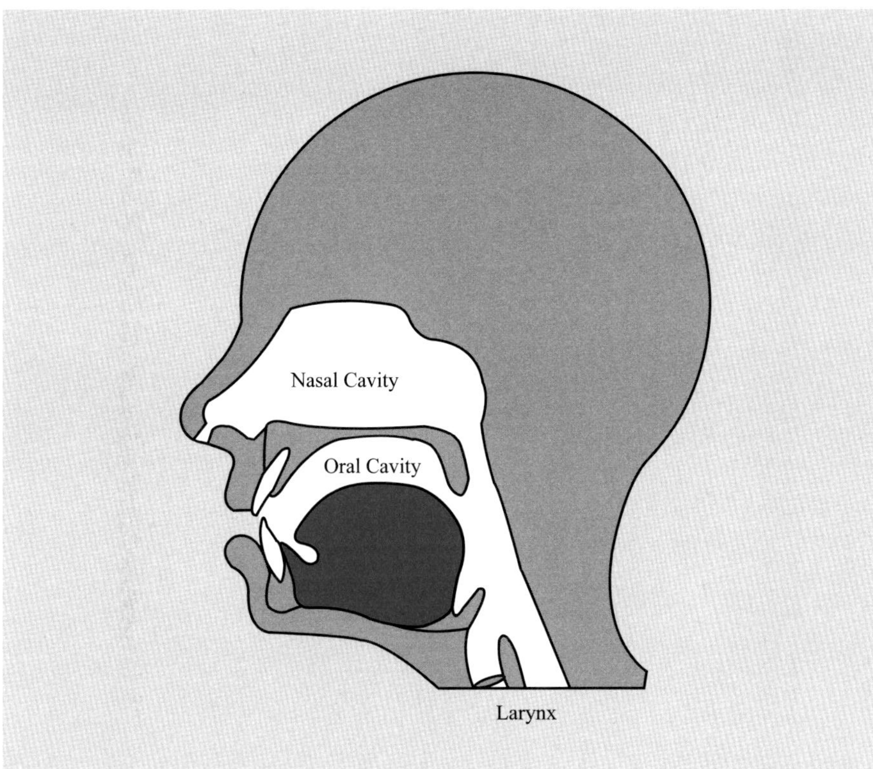

Figure 2. Speech Organs

Principal Vocal Organs

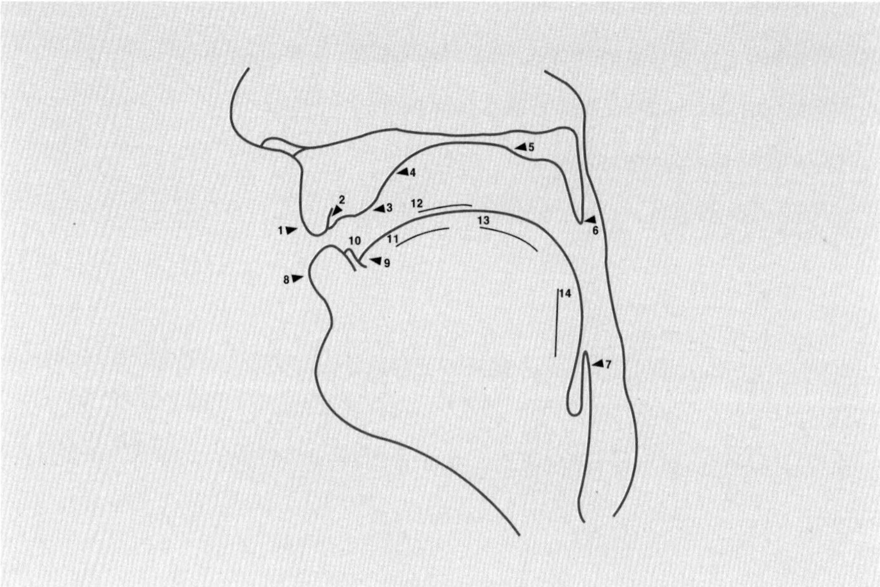

Figure 3. Principal Vocal Organs (Ladefoged, 2006, p. 24)

1. upper lip
2. upper teeth
3. alveolar ridge
4. hard palate
5. soft palate
6. uvula
7. epiglottis
8. lower lip
9. tongue tip
10. tongue blade
11. tongue front
12. tongue center
13. tongue back
14. tongue root

Classification of Speech Sounds

The International Phonetic Alphabet (IPA) is a transcription system that transcribes all speech sounds.

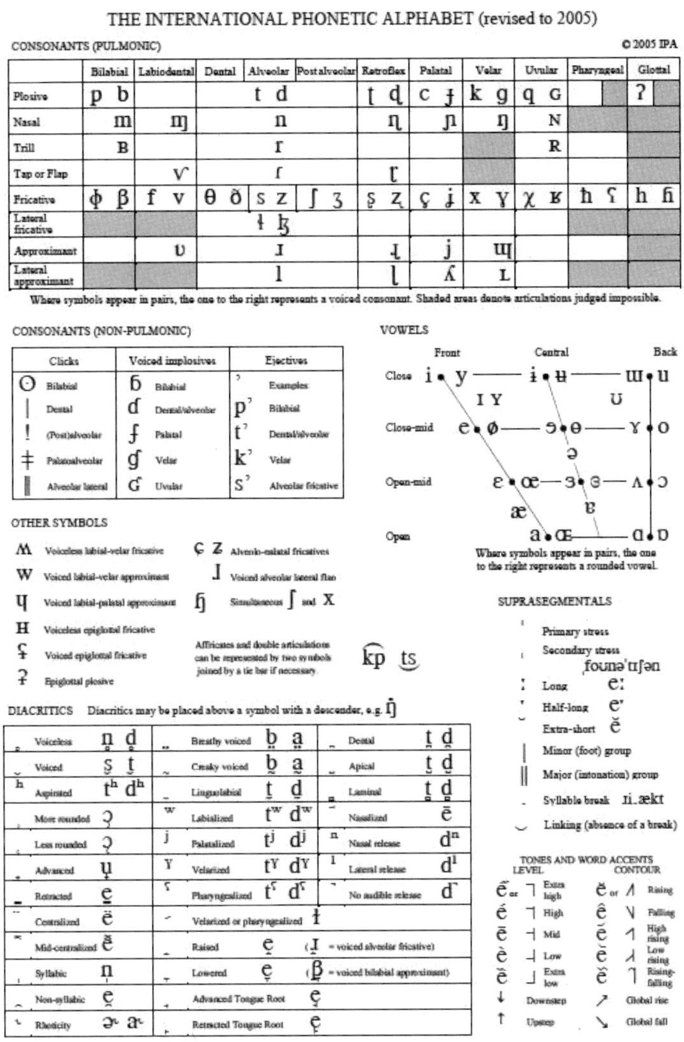

THE INTERNATIONAL PHONETIC ALPHABET (revised to 2005)

CONSONANTS (PULMONIC) © 2005 IPA

	Bilabial	Labiodental	Dental	Alveolar	Postalveolar	Retroflex	Palatal	Velar	Uvular	Pharyngeal	Glottal
Plosive	p b			t d		ʈ ɖ	c ɟ	k ɡ	q ɢ		ʔ
Nasal	m	ɱ		n		ɳ	ɲ	ŋ	ɴ		
Trill	ʙ			r					ʀ		
Tap or Flap		ⱱ		ɾ		ɽ					
Fricative	ɸ β	f v	θ ð	s z	ʃ ʒ	ʂ ʐ	ç ʝ	x ɣ	χ ʁ	ħ ʕ	h ɦ
Lateral fricative				ɬ ɮ							
Approximant		ʋ		ɹ		ɻ	j	ɰ			
Lateral approximant				l		ɭ	ʎ	ʟ			

Where symbols appear in pairs, the one to the right represents a voiced consonant. Shaded areas denote articulations judged impossible.

CONSONANTS (NON-PULMONIC)

Clicks	Voiced implosives	Ejectives
ʘ Bilabial	ɓ Bilabial	ʼ Examples:
ǀ Dental	ɗ Dental/alveolar	pʼ Bilabial
ǃ (Post)alveolar	ʄ Palatal	tʼ Dental/alveolar
ǂ Palatoalveolar	ɠ Velar	kʼ Velar
ǁ Alveolar lateral	ʛ Uvular	sʼ Alveolar fricative

Figure 4. Classification of Speech Sounds

Different Transcription Systems

It is possible that there may be differences in how sounds are transcribed in dictionaries or literatures. The reason is because of the difference in how the sounds are approached. Some put more weight on how the qualities of the sounds differ, whereas some focuse more on the difference in length of the sound.

bead	bid	
[bid]	[bɪd]	quality based
[bi:d]	[bid]	length based

cooed	could	
[kud]	[kʊd]	quality based
[ku:d]	[kud]	length based

Approaches in Learning and Teaching The English Sound System

The English pronunciation has been taught traditionally in analytical manner. Individual sounds are taught, next syllables, then phrases and thought patterns, leading to conversation or discourse. Pronunciation instruction in language classrooms, as a consequence, has been emphasizing the ability to produce sound units. This may make logical sense. However, this is not how languages are experienced. As speakers, people do not think about individual sounds unless there is a breakdown in communication. As listeners, people do not listen to phonemes, but they listen to groups of sound for comprehension. It is now acknowledged that pronunciation needs to be taught in the manner which allows communicative interaction along with mastery of individual sounds.

There are two approaches in teaching and learning pronunciation. One is bottom-up approach, focused on mastering individual sounds and eventually putting them all together. The other is top-down approach which addresses the sound system as natural stream of speech. As grammatical accuracy alone does not achieve communication in speaking, comprehensible pronunciation is not achieved through accurate production of individual sounds. On the other hand, being communicative and having the intent for fluency will not suffice without accuracy. It is clear that even if stresses and intonation is used appropriately, communication can suffer if the individual sounds deviate too far from what is considered standard speech. In this book, a balanced approach to pronunciation will be taken where both top-down and bottom-up approaches will be taken addressing both micro and macro features of pronunciation.

For the application of balanced approach, the model for Blended Learning for Pronunciation, listening, and speaking (BLPls) is suggested for use with this book. The BLPls model presents one-week cycle for teaching and learning English pronunciation along with listening and speaking for English as a Foreign Language (EFL) students. This model has found to be useful and effective, especially in promoting pronunciation and communicative skills through pedagogical instruction and learning experience, individual work, interaction with peer, interaction with teacher, feedback, discussion and reflection, and multimedia components such as voice recording and bulletin board system (BBS) (Yoon, 2011; Yoon & Lee, 2009).

Each cycle of the BLPls model begins with pedagogical instruction that is provided in class. Individual students engage in self-regulated learning with the help of multimedia learning materials. After independent practice in self-regulated learning, the students are to engage in collaborative learning through feedback on BBS through voice recording. At this time, peer feedback and teacher feedback should be provided. When the class meets again, group or class discussion and reflection are made collectively as a new cycle begins with presentation of contents and instruction. Although BLPls model is for blended learning, the process and features suggested in the model can be applied for offline or online classes with slight modifications.

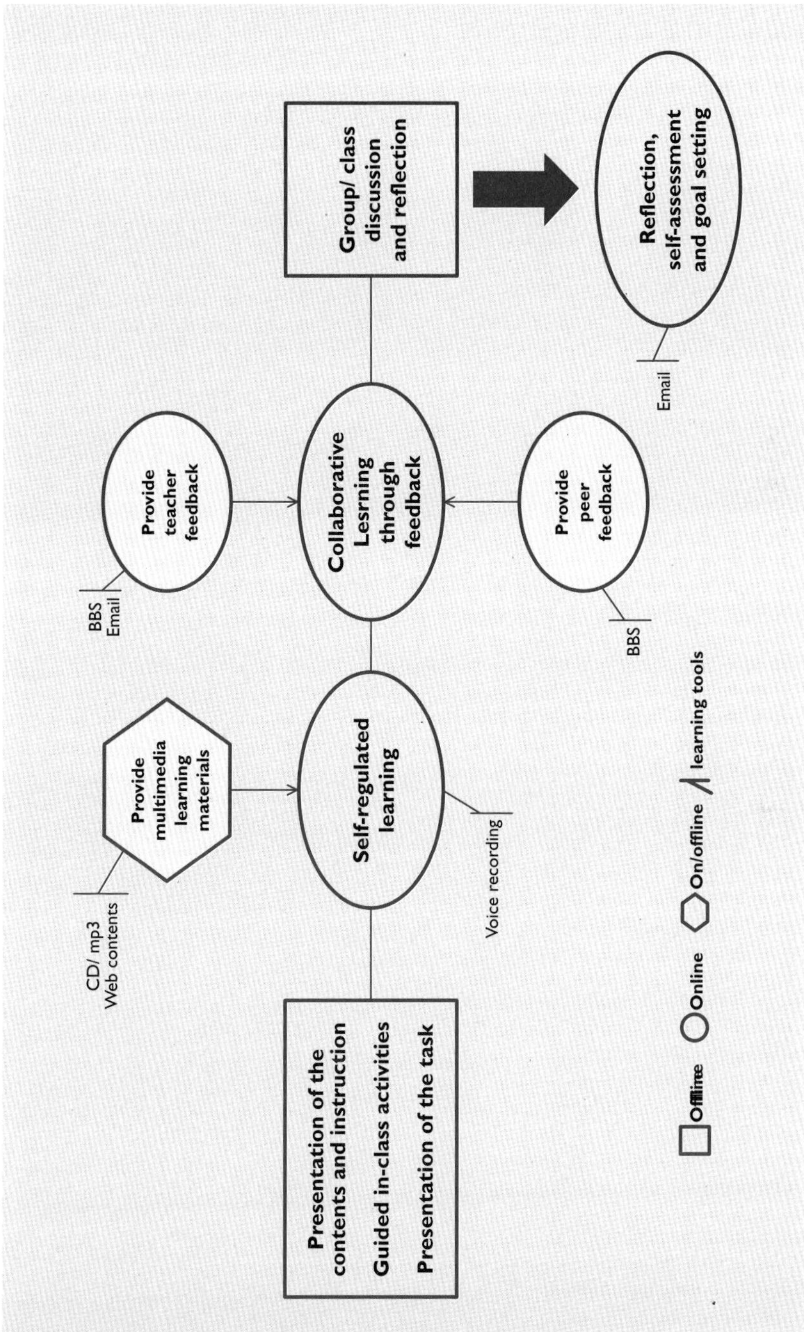

Figure 5. The BLPIs Model (Yoon, 2011)

Unit 2

The Sound System of English

Segments and Suprasegments

Segments

Segment refers to individual sounds. There are two kinds of sounds, consonants and vowels. Vowels and consonants come together to make syllables. In counting how many syllables there are, the number of vowel sounds plays the key role. For example, 'tada' has two vowel sounds, and has two syllables. 'Pencil,' likewise has two syllables. 'Restaurant,' although it seems like there are 4 vowels, there are 3 actual vowel sounds, so there are three syllables.

Suprasegments

Suprasegments, as the name suggests, refer to things that are superimposed on top of segments. It includes stress, pitch, and length.

Stress

Stress is one of the three aspects of rhythm found in speaking. Stress, linking, and intonation work together to create the rhythm of fluent English speakers. Stress can be used to show prominence in a thought group, and it can also mark grammatical category in English.

Example: *ˈoverˌflow (n.) vs. ˌoverˈflow (v.)*

Being able to pronounce sounds accurately is foundational for rhythm, but practicing the rhythm and learning about and practicing stress, linking, and intonation should not wait until all individual sounds are mastered. Rather, they need to go hand in hand.

Pitch

Pitch refers to the highs and lows of sounds. It should be noted that pitch is different from loudness. Pitch is related to the rate of vocal fold vibration. The faster the vocal fold vibrates, the higher the pitch is, and the slower the vibrations, the lower the pitch is.

Pitch Contour

When sounds are pronounced with appropriate pitch, the sounds come together to form pitch contour. Pitch contour can be made linking the changes in pitch for each syllable in a thought group.

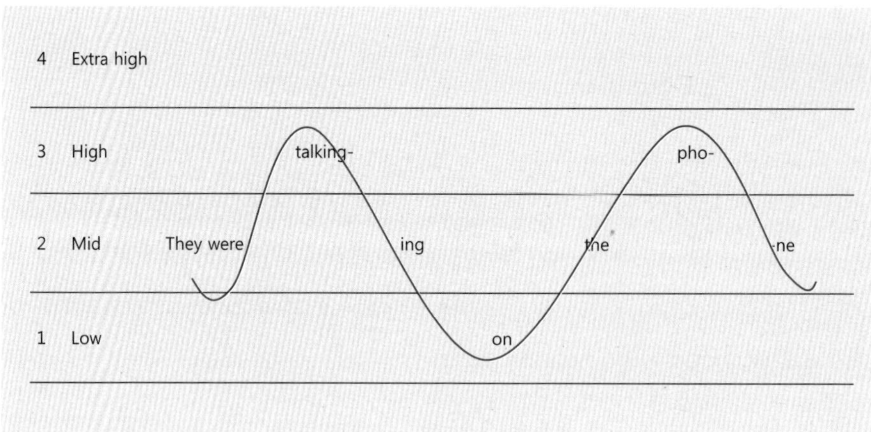

Figure 6. Pitch Contour

When pitch alone signals differences in the meaning of individual words, it is called tone. Chinese, Thai and Vietnamese are tone languages. For example, although /ma/ may seem like one sound, depending on the tone, it can mean different things such as horse or mother. English is not a tonal language. However, the changes in pitch can change the meaning of sentences or thought groups. When the changes in pitch contour changes the meaning of the sentences, it is called intonation.

Syllable Stress

Syllable stress refers to knowing which syllable of a word to say louder and longer than the others. It may seem that there is no specific pattern at to syllable stress; however, there are follow general rules to help the speaker figure out which syllables are stressed. These patterns are based on parts of speech, a category, or on the suffix or prefix of a word.

Example:

Content words	Function words
nouns verbs (except be, have, do) adjectives adverbs (including not) demonstrative pronouns (this, that, these, those) interrogative pronouns (who, when, why, etc.)	articles (a, an, the) simple prepositions (to, of, etc.) personal pronouns (he, it, I, etc.) possessive pronouns (my, his, etc.) relative pronouns (who, that, etc.) conjunctions (and, but, as, if, etc.) the verbs be & have auxiliary verbs (will, can, may, etc.)

Function words and stress
'John or 'Mary should '**GO**. I 'think 'John '**AND** 'Mary should 'go.

Thought Groups

In conversation, speakers to tend to break up long speeches in smaller, manageable groups, called thought groups. The thought groups generally represent a unit of information, and they are signaled by pauses, which is similar to commas and period in writing. Pausing helps the listener to process speech more easily. The most frequent error for language learners is pausing too often. It breaks down the discourse and overloads the listeners, thereby decreasing comprehension.

Prominence

Within each thought group, there is generally one prominent element, a syllable that is stressed. The prominent element can depend on the context, but it generally represents information that is new, in contrast to previous mentioned information, or the most important item in the thought group.

Example:

What are you doing?	I am <u>READ</u>ing.
Who's reading?	<u>I</u> am reading.
Why aren't you reading?!!	I <u>AM</u> reading.

Intonation

The intonation of a sentence is the pattern of pitch changes. Intonation patterns do vary but there are general patterns. Through offering generalized patterns for communicative context, the learners are given an appropriate option among many. It is crucial to provide continued exposure to authentic speech so that the awareness of contextual meaning of intonation choices can be developed.

Intonation plays an important role in English speech rhythm, which is stress-timed. Syllable timed languages like Korean and Japanese differ from stress-timed languages as illustrated in the Figure 7 below.

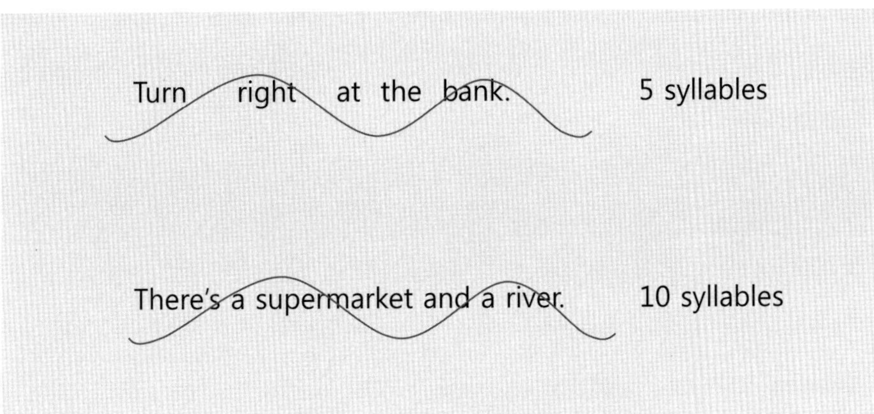

Figure 7. Intonation and Rhythm

Since having too many stresses in a row can cause difficulties in speaking, English avoids having stresses too close together by stress deletion and stress shift. For example, when there are too many content words in a row, starting from the last syllable, every other stress is deleted.

Example:

The 'big 'brown 'bear 'bit 'ten 'white 'mice.

The 'big brown 'bear bit 'ten white 'mice.

It should be noted that unstressed syllables tend to be reduced and shortened. Reduced vowels and shortened sounds can be spoken more quickly, helping speakers to maintain a more regular interval between stressed syllables.

phótogràph	vs.	photógraphy
telépathy	vs.	tèlepáthic
aróma	vs.	àromátic
abólish	vs.	àbolítion
pérson	vs.	persónify
intérrogàte	vs.	ìnterrógative

The following passage is an example of how English is read in regular intervals. Read the passage with a metronome to practice maintaining regular intervals for English intonation pattern. Kinesthetic activities can be useful where learns snap fingers or stand up and take steps to keep beat while practicing the example paragraph.

Listen to the sample recording in female voice then in male voice. Paying attention to the beat and rhythm, practice the following passage.

Example:

'Stresses in 'English 'tend to re 'cur at 'regular 'intervals of 'time. (') It's 'often 'perfectly 'possible to 'tap on the 'stresses in 'time with a 'metronome. (') The 'rhythm can 'even be 'said to de'termine the 'length of the 'pause between 'phrases. (') An 'extra 'tap can be 'put in the 'silence, (') as 'shown by the 'marks with 'in the pa'rentheses. (Ladefoged, 2006)

Further study: English Pronunciation and Korean EFL Learners

Other than aforementioned information such as English being stress-timed and Korean being syllable-timed, there are differences between English and Korean that may cause difficulties in studying English pronunciation.

One is the difference in vowels. There are more vowels in English language that is not used in Korean, which means that it can takes much effort to locate and produce proper English vowel sounds.

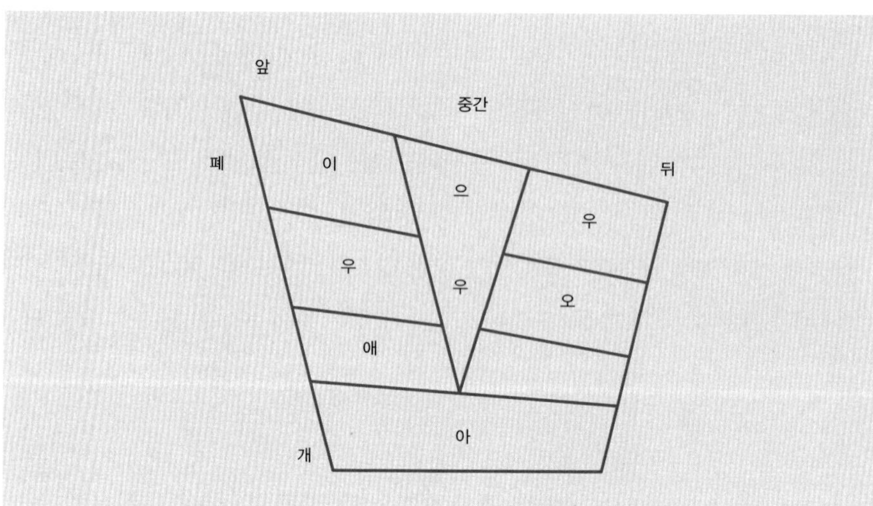

Figure 8. Vowels of Korean Based on Lee (2002)

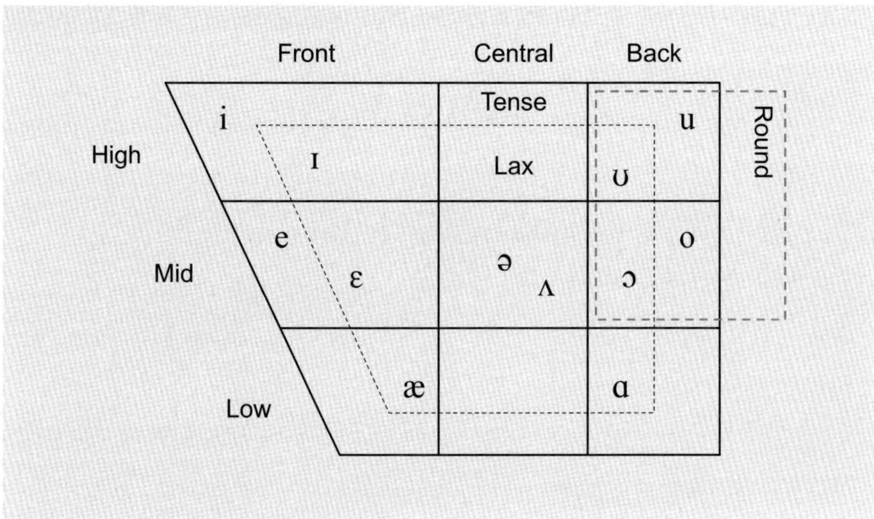

Figure 9. Vowels of English Based on Ladefoged (2006)

In segmental, there are differences as well. The Korean language does not have velarized /l/.

Example:

"life" [laɪf] vs. "file" [faɪɫ]

"feeling" [filɪŋ] vs. "feel" [fiɫ]

Also there are consonants sounds that are used in English but not in Korean. They take more effort to pronounce, and they have caused confusion and negative transfer errors for Korean learners. Sounds such as /f/, /v/, /θ/, /ð/, and /z/ have been pronounced as /p/, /b/, /s/, /d/, /s/, and /ʒ/, respectively, and few examples are provided below.

fine / pine: "파인" /pain/
vase / base: "베이스" /beis/
rock / lock: "락" /lak(ɨ)/
mat / met: "메트" /metɨ/
vision: "비전" /bidʒən/

Another notable difference among many is that Korean language is not concerned with distinguishing the difference between voiced and voiceless consonants, whereas English is. When English words end in voiceless consonants, such as nap and mat, the vowel is pronounced shorter than when these vowels are followed by voiced consonants such as 'nab' and 'mad.'

Unit 3

Intonation

Intonation is one of the most intricate and complicated features of spoken language skills. Not only that is it difficult to conduct researches in intonation due to difficulties in measuring human voice and pitch, there are matters of the differing nature of vowels and consonants, differences between voiced and unvoiced consonants, and emotional aspects of intonation.

Intonation does not occur in separated steps, but like wave, with one tone blending into the next, and there is no rigid rules dictating its use. Since there is no rigid rule, intonation is naturally subjective and relative.

What can be said objectively about intonation is that each thought group has an intonation, which is the pattern of pitch changes. In other words, intonation pattern can change from situation to situation, but there is some generalized patterns that exist. The learners are provided the generalized patterns that suit specific contexts, as an appropriate option, but continued exposure to authentic resources is essential for developing an awareness of contextual meaning of intonation choices.

Example:

Would you like coffee or tea with cream?

Would you like coffee or tea with cream?

Ways to Make Intonation

There are three ways to make intonation. It is through the control of speed, volume, and pitch. Being aware of where to be fast and slow, loud or soft, and high or low, appropriate intonation can be superimposed on syllables.

Reasons for Using Intonation

There are many reasons for using intonation and it can vary from situation to situation. However, the general rule of thumb is that intonation is used to signal the followings in communicative situation.

- New Information
  - What is Jane up to?
  - She's in Mexico.

- Opinion
  - What is that?
  - It sounds like someone's crying.

- Contrasting Information
  - I'm freezing here.
  - Really? I think it's hot!

- Negation: Can't
  - Can you talk?
  - No. I can't.

Unit 4

Word Connection

Linking of American English

Word connection is the linking of multiple sounds. Sometimes they are all blended and shortened as if they are only one word. Native speakers of English all do this naturally, but in most cases, they are not quite aware of doing it. Linking of sounds, along with reduction, is one of the major factors that make listening comprehension difficult. It can cause learners to feel that the native speakers are talking too fast even though the rate of speech is not actually fast at all.

For learners, learning the techniques of connecting sounds can reduce the time spent on practice as time goes by, and it can significantly benefit those who lack fluency in speaking.

Rules for Word Connection

1. Consonant + Vowel: Ending consonant and beginning vowels are connected.

Example: my name is, what is it

2. Consonant + Consonant: When ending consonant and the beginning consonant of the next word are both located in the same category in location of articulation, the sounds are connected into one.

Example: hard times, make cake

	Place of Articulation													
	Bilabial		Labiodental		Interdental		Alveolar		Palatal		Velar		Giottal	
Stop	p	b					t	d			k	g	ʔ	
Fricative			f	v	θ	ð	s	z	ʃ	ʒ			h	
Affricate									tʃ	dʒ				
Nasal		m						n				ŋ		
Lateral Liquid								l						
Glide		(w)										j		

Table 1. Place of Articulation

Consonants can be put into the following categories depending on where the sounds are made.

- behind the teeth : t, d, s, z, ʃ, ʒ, tʃ, dʒ, n, l
- at the lips : p, b, f, v, m, (w)
- in the throat : k, g, ʔ, h, ŋ, j
- others : θ, ð

3. Vowel + Vowel: when a word end with a vowel, and the next word begins in a vowel, natural linking occurs and either slight (y) or (w) sound is produced, depending on the context.

Example: *who is, you are*

4. T, D, S, or Z+ Y: when consonants T, D, S, or Z are linked to Y, the consonants change into different sounds.

t + y = ch

d + y = j

s + y = sh

z + y = zh

Example: *natural, truck, education*

5. TH: Th tends to move around
   - between teeth
   - back of the upper teeth

Example: *th + l: with lemon,*

th + s: with students

Reduction

Reduction is another suprasegmental feature of spoken language which has a strong influence on fluency. Most unstressed syllables are likely to be reduced and shortened. Reduced vowels and segments can be spoken more quickly, helping speakers to maintain a regular interval between stressed syllables.

Example:

- *photograph vs. photography → phot'graph vs. ph'togr'phy*

Example:

- *DOGS EAT BONES.*
- *The DOGS EAT BONES.*
- *The DOGS will EAT BONES.*
- *The DOGS will EAT the BONES.*
- *The DOGS will have EATen the BONES.*

Reduced sounds in words

Beginning: account, agree, alone, enough, opinion
Middle: began, business, general, possible, several, today
Ending: banana, extra, drama

Sentences

I don't know but you can look it up in the dictionary.
The book fell from the table and landed on the carpet.
She doesn't need you to tell her what to do.

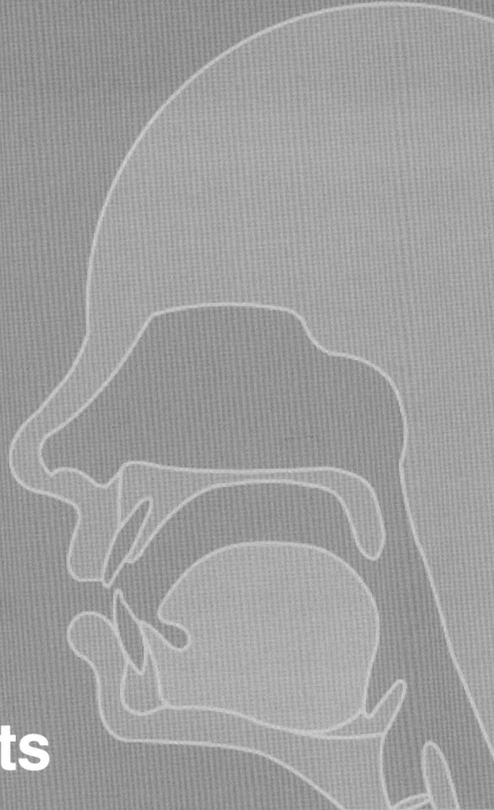

Consonants

Unit 6

Introduction to Consonants

Consonants of English

Consonants can be categorized in three different ways.

1. Manner of articulation: plosive, fricative, affricate, nasal, lateral, and approximant
2. Location of articulation: bilabial, labiodentals, interdental, alveolar, palatoalveolar, palatal, velar, and glottal
3. Vocal folds abduction: voiced or unvoiced

Location / Manner	Bilabial		Labio-Dental		Inter-Dental		Alveolar		Palato-Alveolar		Palatal		Velar		Glottal	
Unvoiced/voiced	uv	v	uv	v	uv	v	uv	v	uv	v	uv	v	uv	v	uv	v
Plosive	p	b					t	d					k	g		
Fricative			f	v	θ	ð	s	z	ʃ	ʒ					h	
Affricate									tʃ	dʒ						
Nasal		m						n						ŋ		
Lateral								l								
Approximant		(w)						r				j		w		

Table 2. The Phonetic Chart of English Consonants, Based on Ladefoged (2006)

Consonants T & D

T	*D*
IPA symbol: /t/ Location: alveolar Manner: stop Unvoiced	IPA symbol: /d/ Location: alveolar Manner: stop Voiced

How sounds are made:

1. The front and sides of the tongue contact the alveolar ridge.
2. Air pressure behind the tongue is released by lowering the tongue, producing noise burst.

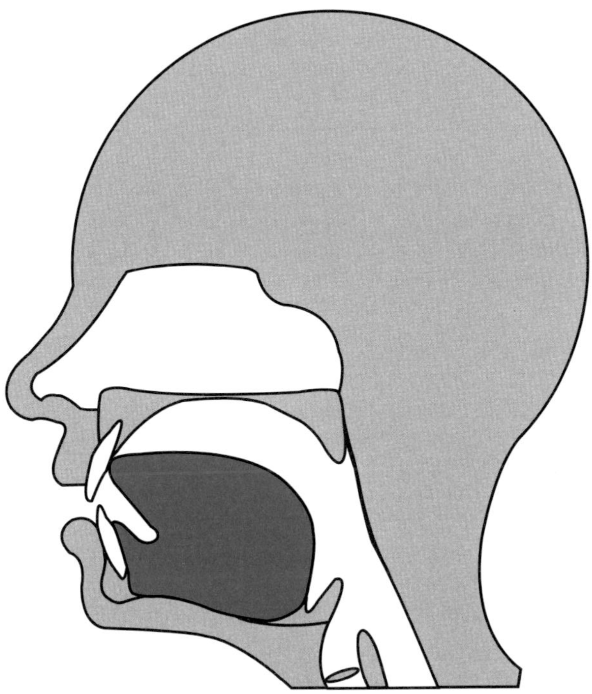

Figure 10. Position of Vocal Organs : Consonants T & D

Track 2 Sounds in Context

Listen and pay attention to how /t/ is pronounced in the beginning, middle, and at the end of words.	Listen and pay attention to how /d/ is pronounced in the beginning, middle, and at the end of words.
Beginning: top, tan, teach Middle: attack, atone Ending: spot, seat	Beginning: dot, doctor Middle: idiom, under Ending: odd, sand

Listen and pay attention to how /t/ and /d/ sounds are pronounced in sentences.

1. Don't forget to fasten the seat belt.
2. The tall people in the front row are blocking my sight.
3. She had a great interview at the international testing society.
4. Can you put butter and strawberry topping on my hot toast?
5. Generally, printed essays looks neater than hand written texts.

Track 3 Six Rules of T

There are general rules that can be applied to the consonant T. Listen and pay close attention to how the consonant T can change depending on what comes before or after it.

1. Beginning T and stressed T: T sounds like /t/.

Tim, tall, test, town, turn, tattoo, material, container

2. Middle T and unstressed T: T becomes reduced.

butter, Saturday, city, visitor, later, battle, computer, battery

3. Ending T: T sound is not released at all.

hot, front, sit, eat, pocket, hurt, salt

4. Unstressed T before N: T sound is held in the throat, then air is released with /n/.

kitten, mitten, curtain, mountain, student, patent

5. N + Reduced Ts with lax vowels: T sound is not pronounced.

Internet, interview, printer, twenty, interfere, interaction

6. Silent T / D: Some consonant clusters cause T or D to become silent.

T: -stle: castle, whistle, hustle

-sten: listen, fasten: glisten

-et: ballet, buffet

often, mustn't, Christmas

D: handsome, Wednesday, handkerchief

Activity 1

Track 4

Listen and check (✓) the location of T, and practice the words aloud.

	Words	Beginning	Middle	Ending
Example	*eastern*		✓	
1	topic			
2	arctic			
3	foster			
4	cast			
5	temporary			
6	crystal			
7	accurate			
8	timid			
9	multiply			
10	create			

Activity 2

Track 5 **Pay close attention to T and read the following sentences aloud. Practice with the recording.**

1. Ending T

It is really not quite right to light night-lights with their slight lights on a light night like tonight.

2. Unstressed T before N

Pretty Kitty Creighton had a cotton batten cat.

The cotton batten cat was bitten by a rat.

3. Middle T and Unstressed T

Betty Botter had some butter, "But," she said, "this butter's bitter.

If I bake this bitter butter, it would make my batter bitter."

4. Intonation with D

If you understand, say "understand."

If you don't understand, say "don't understand."

But if you understand and say "don't understand."

how do I understand that you understand? Understand!?

5. T Combination

A. Did you see the little kitten print satin curtain?

B. Don't eat in front of the computer while surfing the Internet.

C. A celebrity is giving a talk at the Intercontinental hotel.

D. I'd like to visit the castle on Saturday and walk around the garden.

E. He passed the computerized test but failed to do well on the interview.

Activity 3

Track 6

Pay close attention to T and read the following passage aloud. Practice with the recordings.

Introducing Yourself

Hello. Nice to meet you. My name is ________ and I am a student taking a pronunciation class. I don't think my English is terrible, but I feel that having better pronunciation will help me to be a better speaker. I think it's important that people understand me the way I wanted to be understood. I also know that the way I talk can say a lot about what kind of person I am. That is why I am taking my time to learn and improve English pronunciation. I am looking forward to a great learning experience.

Further Study: -ed endings

Track 7

Listen and pay attention to how –ed ending sound is pronounced differently depending on the context.

d	t	id
When –ed comes after voiced consonant sound other than /d/	When –ed comes after unvoiced consonant sound other than /t/	When –ed comes after /t/ or /d/
judged inspired turned	looked crossed picked	crafted rested faded

Activity 1

Track 8

Listen for the –ed endings and check (✓) the appropriate box, and practice the words aloud.

	Verbs	-d	-t	-id
Example	*crossed*		✓	
1	hated			
2	watched			
3	yelled			
4	invited			
5	worked			
6	married			
7	saved			
8	folded			
9	created			
10	learned			
11	touched			
12	rocked			

Activity 2

Listen for the –ed endings and circle the appropriate sound in the parenthesis. Then practice reading the sentences aloud.

Example: *She looked refreshed when she walked out of the spa.*

([d] / t / id) *(d / [t] / id)*

1. The dog reached the corner, turned left and ran away.

   (d / t / id) (d / t / id)

2. The boy yelled at his classmate who cheated on the test.

   (d / t / id) (d / t / id)

3. After I invited them to dinner, I vacuumed and cleaned the house.

   (d / t / id) (d / t / id) (d / t / id)

4. He folded the laundry while she washed the dishes, wiped the counter.

   (d / t / id) (d / t / id) (d / t / id)

Unit 8

Consonant L

L

IPA symbol: /l/
Location: alveolar
Manner: liquid
Voiced

How sounds are made:

1. Touch the tip of your tongue to the inside of your front teeth.
2. Lower the sides of your tongue.
3. Do not round your lips.
4. Push air out over the sides of your tongue.

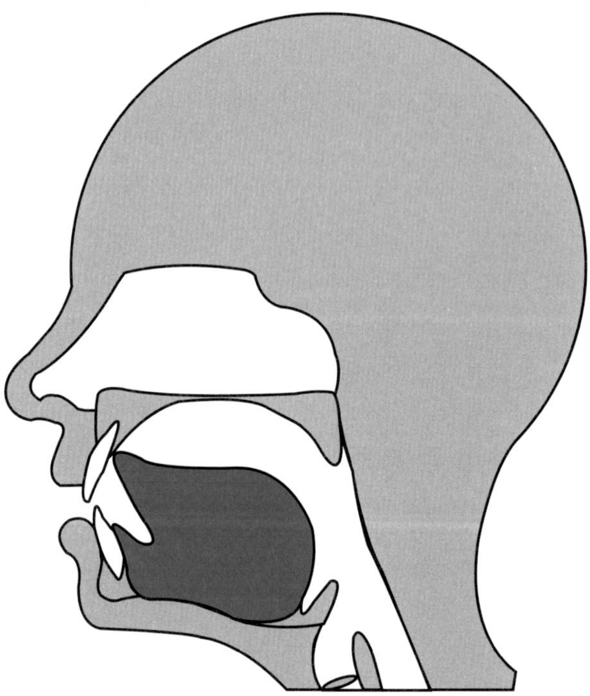

Figure 11. Position of Vocal Organs : Consonant L

Track 10

Sounds in Context

Listen and pay attention to how /l/ is pronounced in the beginning, middle, and at the end of words.

Beginning: like, least, land
Middle: relative, prologue, yellow
Ending: pull, fall, fill

Listen and pay attention to how /l/ is pronounced in sentences.

Listen and pay attention to how /l/ is pronounced in sentences.

1. Lovely ladies walked around the pool.
2. Stealing food is almost always due to hunger.
3. The yellow leaf is falling slowly from the wall.

There are general rules that can be applied to the consonant L. Listen and play close attention to how the consonant L can change depending on the context.

Track 11

Dark L: When a vowel is followed by an ending /l/, the back of the tongue is raised towards velar, which causes velarization of /l/.

pool, steal, crawl, fool, real

Silent L: Some consonant clusters cause /l/ to become silent.

-ld: could, should, would
-lf: half, calf
-lk: walk, talk, chalk
-lm: Salmon, calm, palm, alm

Activity 1

1. Read the following words aloud paying attention to /l/ sound.

1. land	lend	lily	laid	lost	lull	loose
2. falling	filler	fly	failed	foliage	fullest	foolish
3. tall	tell	till	tail	tour	tulip	tool
4. ran	real	rill	rail	role	rule	rooster

Track 12

2. Underline the words containing silent L and practice with the recording.

Example: *plumb* *palm* *plunder* *plump*

1. shoal	shoulder	should	shelf
2. clam	calm	calamity	calcium
3. almost	alarmed	allergy	allotted
4. salamander	salient	supply	salmon
5. follow	fold	folk	file

Activity 2

Track 13 **Listen to the recording and choose the appropriate words.**

Example: *The lovely rose is (glowing / growing).*

1. Your answer is (wrong / long).

2. On Sundays, I take time out to (pray / play).

3. It seems as if she is (boring / bowling).

4. Why don't we (work / walk) for about an hour before dinner.

5. His dream is to become a (pirate / pilot).

6. Be careful not to walk on the (grass / glass).

Activity 3

Track 14 **Listen and fill in the blanks. Practice reading the passage aloud.**

A Walk in the Park

I took a ________ down the park. It was ________ cold and I was wearing the ________ clothes. On the road, I found a ________. I realized that it was a ________ one. I didn't want an extra ________ so I didn't pick it up. I continued to ________ on my stroll. When I came to a ________, I decided to add it to my ________. By the time I came home, it was not ________ anymore but I was ________ tired.

Unit 9

Consonant R

R

IPA symbol: /r/
Location: palatal
Manner: liquid
Voiced

How sounds are made:

1. Tongue tip points to the palate.
2. The sides of the tongue are raised.
3. Lips are slightly rounded.

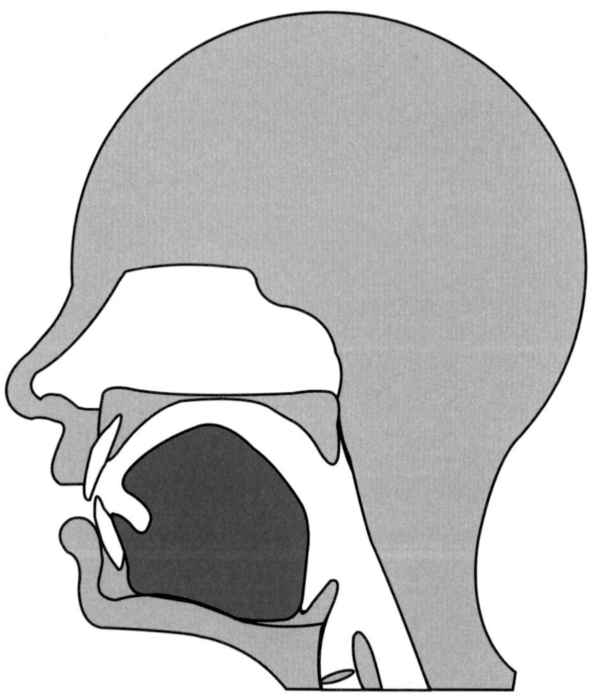

Figure 12. Position of Vocal Organs : Consonant R

Track 15

Sounds in Context

Listen and pay attention to how /r/ is pronounced in the beginning, middle, and at the end of words.

Beginning: Red, Read, Round
Middle: Sarah, carry, primary
Ending: taller, color, far

Listen and pay attention to how /rl/ is pronounced.

girl, pearl, world, sirloin, furl

Listen and pay attention to how /r/ is pronounced in sentences.

1. Red is her favorite color.
2. He dreamed of a world full of happiness.
3. Sarah received pearl earrings for her birthday.

Activity 1

Track 16 **Listen and check (✓) the appropriate box, and practice the words aloud.**

Example	***tower***		***towel***	✓
1	fire		fire	
2	heel		hear	
3	teal		tear	
4	peer		peel	
5	right		light	
6	lead		read	

Activity 2

Track 17 **Listen and circle the word you hear, and practice the words aloud.**

Example: *He is an avid (reader / leader).*

1. (Law / Raw) is there to be kept, not broken

2. The (climb / crime) was not only terrifying but really tiring.

3. When the tall player threw the ball, it hit the (limb / rim) and went in.

4. One problem with bringing in stray animals is that they might have (fleas / freeze).

5. Did you see how much Arnold's (belly / berry) has grown over the summer?

Activity 3

Track 18 **Pay close attention to consonants L and R and read the following story aloud. Practice with the recording.**

Little Red Riding Hood

A long, long time ago, a girl called Little Red Riding Hood went to visit her grandmother. While Little Red Riding Hood strolled along the lovely country road, the big bad wolf came and swallowed Granny. Then he put on Granny's cap, got into Granny's bed, and covered up with blankets. Little Red Riding Hood arrived and said, "Granny, what big ears you have!" and the wolf replied, "All the better to hear you with, my dear!" Then she said, "Granny, what big eyes you have!" and the wolf replied, "All the better to see you with, my dear!" Then Little Red Riding Hood said, "Granny, what big teeth you have!" and the wolf replied, "All the better to eat you with, my dear!" Then the wolf swallowed up the girl. Luckily, a passing by lumberjack saw it all. He battled the wolf and rescued Little Red Riding Hood and Granny. Later, three of them drank lemonade together and lived happily ever after.

Track 19 ***Tongue Twisters***

1. Roberta ran rings around the Roman ruins.
2. Literary literature literally lasts a really long time.
3. It's the right light with the glimmer in the mirror.
4. Laura and Larry rarely lull their rural roosters to sleep.

Consonant TH

TH

IPA symbol: /θ/ Location: dental Manner: fricative Unvoiced	IPA symbol: /ð/ Location: dental Manner: fricative Voiced

How sounds are made:

1. Tongue tip touches the bottom of the upper teeth.
2. Bring the tongue in and let a puff of air flow out.

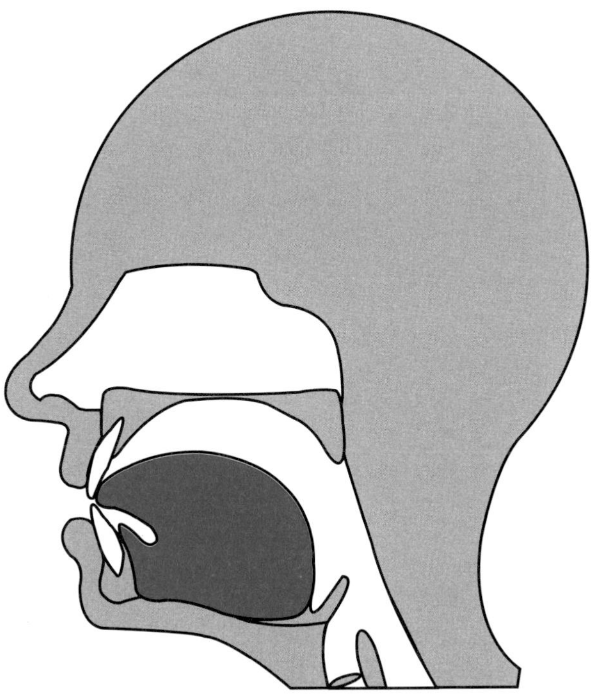

Figure 13. Position of Vocal Organs : Consonant TH

Track 20 Sounds in Context

Listen and pay attention to how /θ/ is pronounced in the beginning, middle, and at the end of words.	Listen and pay attention to how /ð/ is pronounced in the beginning, middle, and at the end of words.
Beginning: think, three, thermometer Middle: authentic, athlete Ending: mouth, youth	Beginning: there, though Middle: mother, brother Ending: bathe, breathe

Listen and pay attention to how /θ/ and /ð/ sounds are pronounced in sentences.

1. The youthful teenager kept breathing through his mouth.
2. He pushed the thumb tack with the thick of his thumb.
3. Thirty thousand three hundred thirty three athletes are running through the theatre.

Activity 1

Track 21

You will hear two words. Listen and check (✓) whether they sound the same or different.

Example	*Same*		*Different*	✓	***sought / thought***
1	Same		Different		**?/?**
2	Same		Different		**?/?**
3	Same		Different		**?/?**
4	Same		Different		**?/?**
5	Same		Different		**?/?**
6	Same		Different		**?/?**

Activity 2

Track 22 **Listen and fill in the blanks. Then practice the sentences aloud.**

Example: *Either you are with us or you are with them.*

1. That man is healthy, ________________, and well-educated.

2. I need to take the temperature, but I can't find the ______________.

3. Take the thirty little sweaters to the _______ _________ mother showed you on ________________.

4. They all ________________ that they were utterly lost until those hikers showed up in their ________________.

5. These ________________ tend to be active at night, but some in ________________ hemisphere thrive in the day time, too.

Activity 3

Track 23 **Pay close attention to TH and read the following passage aloud. Practice with the recording.**

The recording of this passage can be found in The Speech Accent Archive (http://accent.gmu.edu).

Please call Stella. Ask her to bring these things with her from the store: Six spoons of fresh snow peas, five thick slabs of blue cheese, and maybe a snack for her brother Bob. We also need a small plastic snake and a big toy frog for the kids. She can scoop these things into three red bags, and we will go meet her Wednesday at the train station.

To compare your recording with nonnative English speakers of Korean background, go to:
http://accent.gmu.edu/browse_language.php?function=find&language=korean

To compare your recording with nonnative speakers of different background, go to:
http://accent.gmu.edu/browse_language.php

You may need to download Quicktime plug-in (http://www.apple.com/quicktime/download/) to play the sound files.

Track 24

Tongue Twisters

1. They both have thirty-three thick thimbles to thaw.
2. Lesser weather never weathered lesser wetter weather.
3. Thank the other three brothers on their father's mother's brother's side.
4. The thirty three thieves thought that they thrilled the throne throughout Thursday.

Consonants F & V

F	*V*
IPA symbol: /f/ Location: dental Manner: fricative Unvoiced	IPA symbol: /v/ Location: dental Manner: fricative Voiced

How sounds are made:

1. The upper teeth touch the inside of the lower lip.
2. As the air flows out, friction is created.

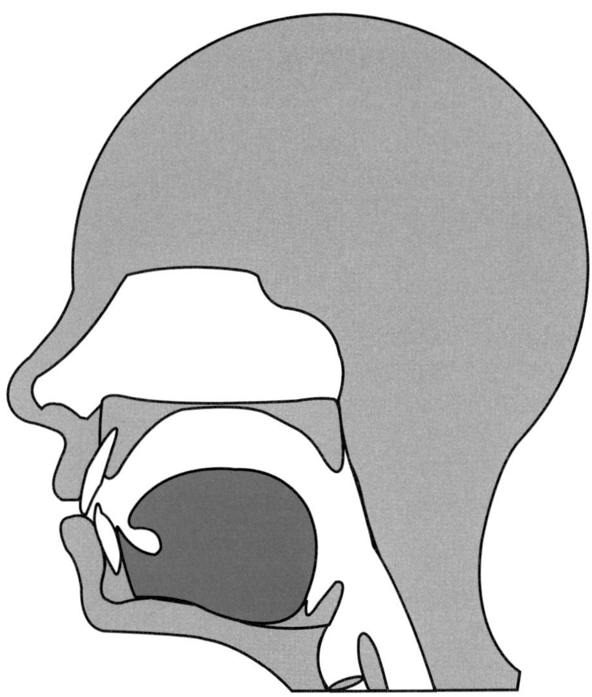

Figure 14. Position of Vocal Organs : Consonants F & V

Track 25

Sounds in Context

Listen and pay attention to how /f/ is pronounced in the beginning, middle, and at the end of words.	Listen and pay attention to how /v/ is pronounced in the beginning, middle, and at the end of words.
Beginning: fan, free, forest Middle: offer, prefer, affect Ending: cough, enough, laugh	Beginning: van, vast, victory Middle: over, avenge, ivory Ending: cave, have, leave

Listen and pay attention to how /f/ and /v/ sounds are pronounced in sentences.
1. Her minivan overheated when the fan stopped working. 2. The officer offered him two choices, to stay or to leave. 3. If you have severe cough and high fever, visit a doctor's office soon.

Activity 1

Track 26 **Listen and check (✓) the word you hear.**

Example	*often*		*oven*	✓	*open*	
1	fan		Fran		pan	
2	ferry		very		fairy	
3	half		halve		help	
4	pew		few		view	
5	ripe		life		live	
6	self		save		safe	

Activity 2

Track 27

Fill in the blanks with the words provided in the box. Then practice the sentences aloud.

Example: *The view from the window is quite nice.*

1. Would you like a _______ or a quarter of this apple?

2. Cover your mouth when you _______, especially if you are sick.

3. When you _______, please turn _______ the computers and the lights.

4. It is recommended that you exercise _______, at least three times a week.

5. The youth _______ his seat to an elderly lady who was carrying a _______ load.

leave	few	happy	laugh
live	cough	~~view~~	often
of	offered	calf	half
heavy	free	off	self

Activity 3

Track 28 **Listen and fill in the blanks. Then paying close attention to F and V, practice the passage aloud.**

Frank and his wife, Olivia, ______ to Florida for their summer ________. They had delicacies made from fish and ___________ ___________. When they got back home to Nevada, they couldn't _______ _______ their old clothes anymore. They've gained ________ ________ over two weeks. They were horrified. Frank felt fat and Olivia thought she ________ from obesity at first. But soon, they decided that since they had such a _________________time that they decided to _________________ and go shopping for new clothes instead.

Track 29 ***Tongue Twisters***

1. Freshly fried fresh fish flesh.
2. Five fast fish floundered in the fast flowing flood.
3. Fred the finicky flamingo failed to find food fit to feed from.
4. A bevy of beautiful bovines eat vines and berries.
5. Eleven benevolent elephants vowed vengeance very vehemently.

Unit 12

Consonants P & B

P	B
IPA symbol: **/p/** Location: bilabial Manner: stop Unvoiced	IPA symbol: **/b/** Location: bilabial Manner: stop Voiced

How sounds are made:

1. Lips are closed so that upper and lower lips are touching.
2. As the lips separate, a burst of air is let out.

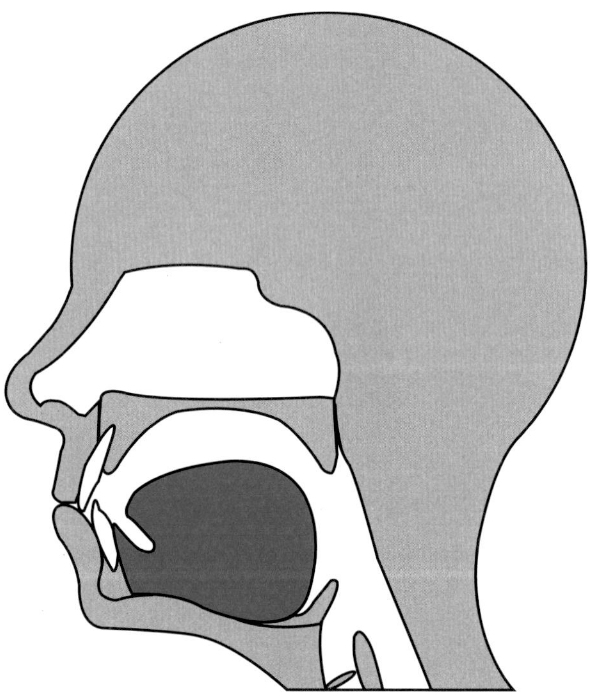

Figure 15. Position of Vocal Organs : Consonants P & B

Track 30 Sounds in Context

Listen and pay attention to how /p/ is pronounced in the beginning, middle, and at the end of words.	Listen and pay attention to how /b/ is pronounced in the beginning, middle, and at the end of words.
Beginning: pan, pride Middle: apple, computer Ending: stop, cap	Beginning: ban, bride Middle: abandon, combine Ending: cab, grab

Listen and pay attention to how /p/ and /b/ sounds are pronounced in sentences.

1. Paul was not able to fix his computer.
2. The proud bride stopped to buy some apples.
3. I got on the cab to go grab some crabs at the beach.

Listen and pay attention to silent /p/ and /b/.

Silent P/B
-mb-(ending): lamb, bomb, comb

psy: psychology, psyche
cupboard, doubt, receipt

*ph=f

Activity 1

Track 31

You will hear three words. Put a check (✓) in the box where the word sounds different from the other two words.

	A	B	C
Example	*pray*	*pray*	*fray (✓)*
1			
2			
3			
4			
5			
6			

Track 32 **Listen and choose the word you hear. Practice the sentences aloud.**

Example: *There is a (bear / pear) in the large tree.*

1. Can you get the pen from the (back / pack)?

2. This (beach / peach) is great. I love it.

3. Let's get a (cap / cab) for the baseball game.

4. I heard that (they've earned / they burned) the diploma last semester.

Activity 3

Track 33 **Pay close attention to consonants P and B and practice reading the passage aloud.**

Weather Forecast

Good evening and welcome to the Wednesday's weather report. Well, we're going to have mixed weather across the country. The cold front that's been moving north may bring snow in the upper region tomorrow. There's a strong chance the snow will continue until Friday.

Another cold front is moving south-west and should arrive on the west coast tomorrow evening. We can expect cold winds and rain late Friday afternoon. It's possible that this rain will continue overnight, until Saturday.

On the east coast, we are expecting a slight rise in temperatures, from today's high of seven degrees to high as fifteen degrees. But the mild weather won't last very long. The cold front affecting the rest of the country will reach the east by Sunday evening.

Track 34 ***Tongue Twisters***

1. Bright blows the broom on the brook's bare brown banks.
2. The bleak breeze blights the bright blue blossom.
3. Peter Piper picked a peck of pickled peppers.
4. Did Peter Piper pick a peck of pickled peppers?

Consonants S & Z

S	Z
IPA symbol: /s/ Location: alveolar Manner: fricative Unvoiced	IPA symbol: /z/ Location: alveolar Manner: fricative Voiced

How sounds are made:

1. The tongue is raised toward the upper teeth.
2. As the air flows out, friction is created.

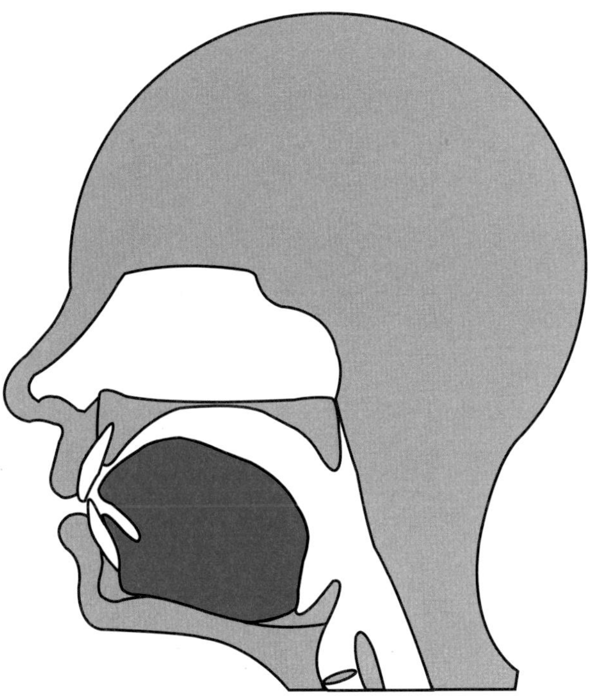

Figure 16. Position of Vocal Organs : Consonants S & Z

Track 35

Sounds in Context

Listen and pay attention to how /s/ is pronounced in the beginning, middle, and at the end of words.	Listen and pay attention to how /z/ is pronounced in the beginning, middle, and at the end of words.
Beginning: sorry, sad, snow, start Middle: ask, producer, massive Ending: pass, grass	Beginning: zebra, zoo Middle: easy, position, grazed Ending: motives, alternatives, loves

Listen and pay attention to how /s/ and /z/ sounds are pronounced in sentences.

1. The sad zebra was grazing on the grass.
2. Jack and Zack asked the producer to switch their roles.
3. The girls started ski lessons when they were six years old.

The Letter X

Listen and pay attention to how X can sound differently depending on the context.

KS: followed by unvoiced consonants
extra, experience, exciting, excavate, exterminate, excellent

GS: followed by a vowel and usually stressed on the second syllable
exam. example, exit, exude, exaggerate, exactly, executive

Activity 1

Track 36 **Listen and circle (○) the word you hear. Practice them aloud.**

Example: (*sip*) *sip*

1. prices prizes
2. racing raising
3. niece knees
4. peace peas
5. Jack Zack
6. Sue zoo
7. Jane zane
8. jip zip

Activity 2

Track 37

Listen and fill in the blanks. Then practice them aloud.

1. If you don't take the _____ I give you, I can't _____ you. **(advice/ advise)**

2. The coffee shop _____ to my house _____ early. **(closes/close)**

3. The _____ you have to pay is worth the _____. **(prize/price)**

4. I don't know for sure but I think _____ is at the _____. **(Sue/ zoo)**

5. Your button is _____, you might _____ it if it falls off. **(lose/loose)**

Activity 3

Track 38

Pay close attention to /s/ and /z/, and practice the following speech aloud.

An Excerpt from Gettysburg Address by Abraham Lincoln

But, in a larger sense, we cannot dedicate, we cannot consecrate, we cannot hallow this ground. The brave men, living and dead who struggled here have consecrated it far above our poor power to add or detract. The world will little note nor long remember what we say here, but it can never forget what they did here. It is for us the living rather to be dedicated here to the unfinished work which they who fought here have thus far so nobly advanced. It is rather for us to be here dedicated to the great task remaining before us -- that from these honored dead we take increased devotion to that cause for which they gave the last full measure of devotion – that we here highly resolve that these dead shall not have died in vain, that this nation under God shall have a new birth of freedom, and that government of the people, by the people, for the people shall not perish from the earth.

* For authentic sample, go to:

http://www.americanrhetoric.com/speeches/gettysburgaddress.htm

Further Study: -S Endings

Track 39

Listen and pay attention to how –s ending sound is pronounced differently depending on the context.

z	s	iz
When s comes after voiced consonants other than /z/ and /ʒ/	When s comes after unvoiced consonants other than /s/, /ʃ/, /tʃ/, /dʒ/	When s comes after /ʒ/, /dʒ/, /s/, /ʃ/, /tʃ/, /dʒ/
shoes cans players	pants socks lips	glasses pushes switches

Activity 1

Track 40

Listen for the –s endings and check the appropriate box, and practice the words aloud.

	Verbs	-z	-s	-iz
Example	*gasses*			✓
1	clocks			
2	pencils			
3	classes			
4	balloons			
5	sheets			
6	pickles			
7	purses			
8	ships			
9	units			
10	axes			
11	checks			
12	bags			
13	scissors			
14	students			

Activity 2

Track 41

Listen for the –s endings and circle the appropriate sound in the parenthesis. Then practice reading the sentences aloud.

Example: *Jenny's brothers all wear blue jeans.*

(s / [z] / iz) *(s / [z] / iz)*

1. She never watches horror movies without her dogs.

(s / z / iz) (s / z / iz) (s / z / iz)

2. There are axes in her trunk as well as spikes and screws.

(s / z / iz) (s / z / iz) (s / z / iz)

3. The students like the chapter on plants and animals.

(s / z / iz) (s / z / iz) (s / z / iz)

4. He examines the sights carefully, including the exits and entrances.

(s / z / iz) (s / z / iz) (s / z / iz)

Consonants /ʃ/ & /ʒ/

SH	ZH
IPA symbol: /ʃ/ Location: palato-alveolar Manner: fricative Unvoiced	IPA symbol: /ʒ/ Location: palato-alveolar Manner: fricative Voiced

How sounds are made:

1. Tongue tip and blade are raised to touch the side of the teeth.
2. The center of the tongue is lowered.
3. Air flows out of the lowered center of the tongue.

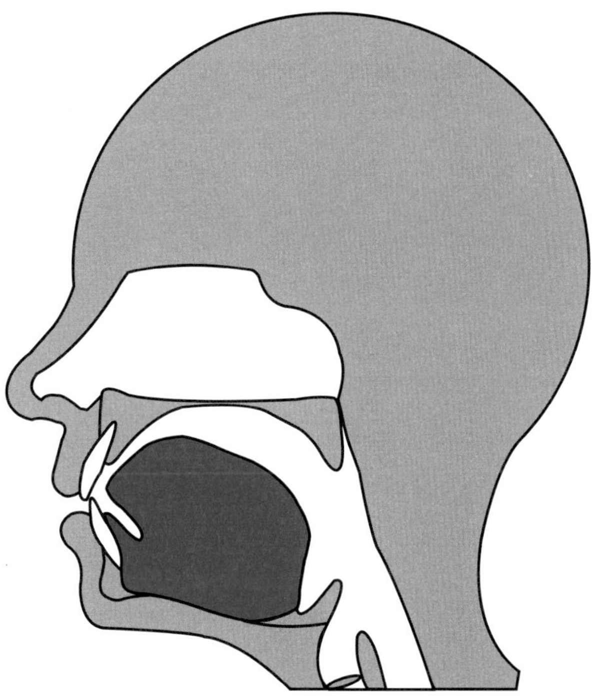

Figure 17. Position of Vocal Organs : Consonant /ʃ/ & /ʒ/

Track 42

Sounds in Context

Listen and pay attention to how /ʃ/ is pronounced in the beginning, middle, and at the end of words.	Listen and pay attention to how /ʒ/ is pronounced in the beginning, middle, and at the end of words.
Beginning: shoe, shadow Middle: mission, dasher Ending: fish, cash, smash	Beginning: n/a Middle: regime, version Ending: rage

Listen and pay attention to how /ʃ/ and /ʒ/ sounds are pronounced in sentences.
1. Fishing is a hobby shared by many outdoor lovers. 2. The mission was aborted when they ran out of cash. 3. The other version of the movie showed a vision of diversion.

Activity 1

Track 43

Listen and check (✓) the word you hear.

	/s/		/ʃ/	
Example	*Sue*	✓	*shoe*	
1	Sam		sham	
2	sop		shop	
3	sear		shear	
4	rust		rushed	
5	lease		leash	

Activity 2

Track 44

Listen and circle the word you hear then practice reading the sentences aloud.

Example: *Seizures / Scissors are dangerous at times.*

1. We saw a dog (watching / washing) cars.

2. They were planning to (chew / shoe / sue) him.

3. I saw a (batch / badge / bash) on my neighbor's yard.

4. He was (leasing / leashing / leaching) the dog when she walked in the door.

Activity 3

Track 45

Pay close attention to /ʃ/ and /ʒ/, and read the following passage aloud. Practice with the recording.

My Hobby

My hobby is going to the shopping mall. I used to go fishing at the seashore on the weekend, but now I spend time at the shopping mall. I'm not rich, so I have to choose carefully when I charge my credit card. Last weekend, I went to the shopping center with my cousin, George, from Virginia. We bought matching shirts. Then we watched a movie about Trojan soldiers and went for desserts. We had a good time, and I envision an even more pleasurable shopping experience when the sales begin next month.

Unit 15

Other Consonants M, N , NG, H, K & G

Nasal

M

IPA symbol: /m/
Place: bilabial
Manner: nasal
Voiced

How sounds are made:

1. The upper lip and the lower lip come together.
2. Nasal passage opens and resonance in the nasal passage can be felt.

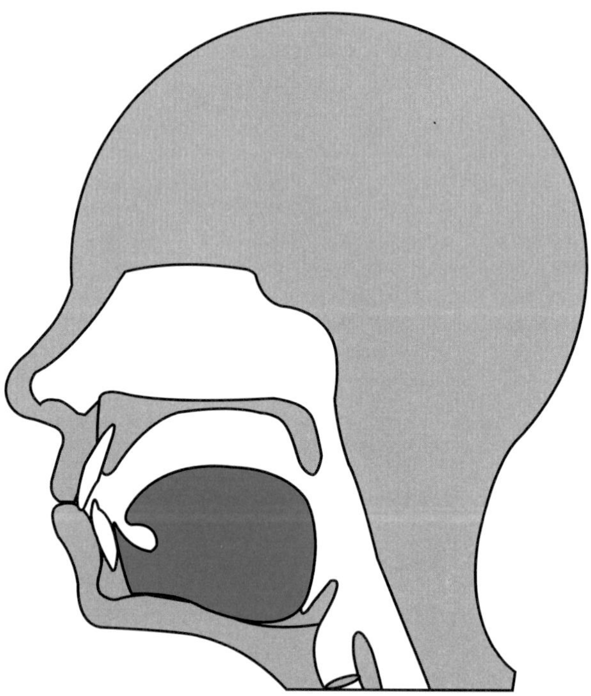

Figure 18. Position of Vocal Organs : Consonant M

Track 46

Sounds in Context

Listen and pay attention to how /m/ sound is pronounced in sentences.

1. Merry Mary cared much for her lambs.
2. Most men like machines and motorcycles.
3. The math club members must prepare for math competition.

N

IPA symbol: /n/
Place: alveolar
Manner: nasal
Voiced

How sounds are made:

1. Tongue tip touches the alveolar ridge.
2. Air flow out of the nose and the nasal passage.

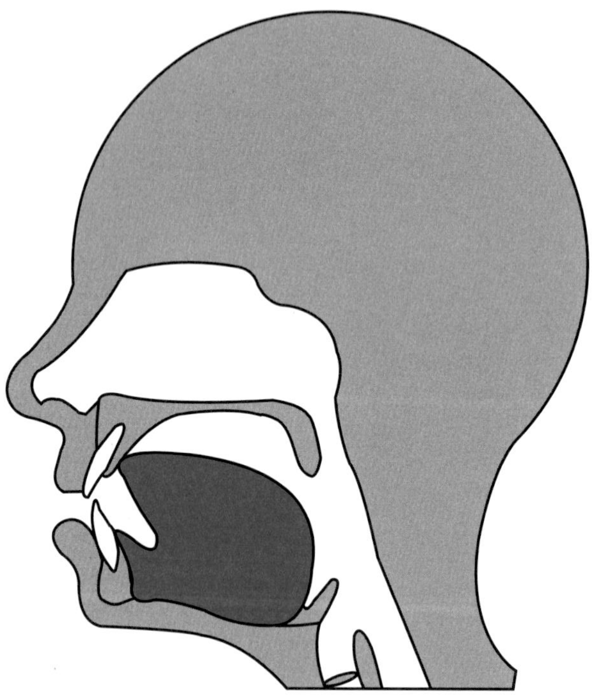

Figure 19. Position of Vocal Organs : Consonant N

Track 47

Sounds in Context

Listen and pay attention to how /n/ sound is pronounced in sentences.

1. No one went the gym after nine at night.
2. I was nervous to see Nancy angry at the dinner.
3. Don't you know it is dangerous to run through the snow bank?

NG

IPA symbol: /ŋ/
Place: velar
Manner: nasal
Voiced

How sounds are made:

1. The back of the tongue touches velum.
2. The air flows out of the nasa passage.

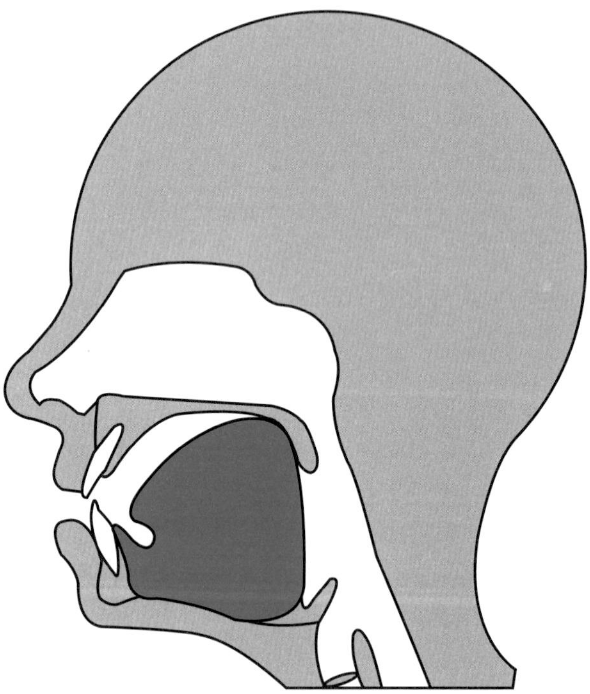

Figure 20. Position of Vocal Organs : Consonant NG

Track 48

Sounds in Context

Listen and pay attention to how /ŋ/ sound is pronounced in sentences.

1. Young King Kong ring bells and sing songs.
2. When I was younger, English classes seemed longer.
3. The king was stronger than the strongest man in England.

Velar

H

IPA symbol: /h/
Location: glottal
Manner: fricative
Unvoiced

How sounds are made:

Epiglottis opens and the larynx contracts as air flows out.

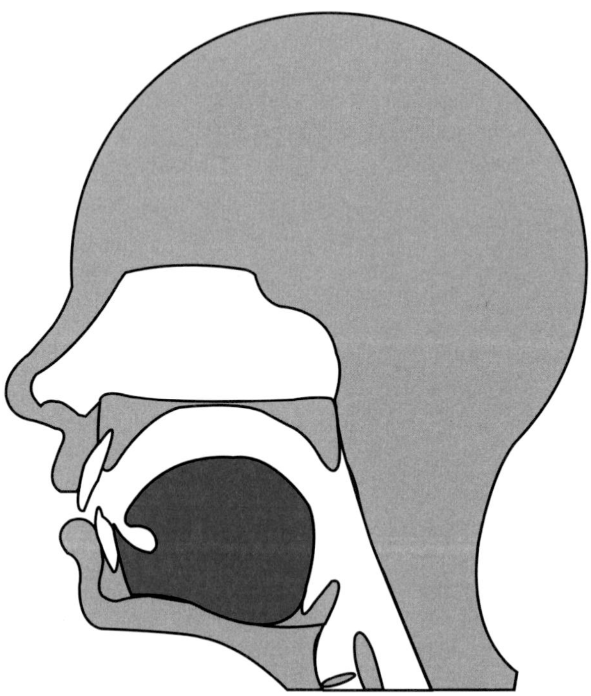

Figure 21. Position of Vocal Organs : Consonant H

Track 49

Sounds in Context

Listen and pay attention to how /h/ sound is pronounced in sentences.

1. Hurry and help her put helmet on her head.
2. Helen felt happier and healthier eating at home.
3. Half an hour in the summer heat can cause heat stroke.

Glottal

K	G
IPA symbol: /h/ Location: velar Manner: stop Unvoiced	IPA symbol: /g/ Location: velar Manner: stop Unvoiced

How sounds are made:

1. The back of the tongue touches the velum.
2. The tongue separates and there is a sudden burst of air.

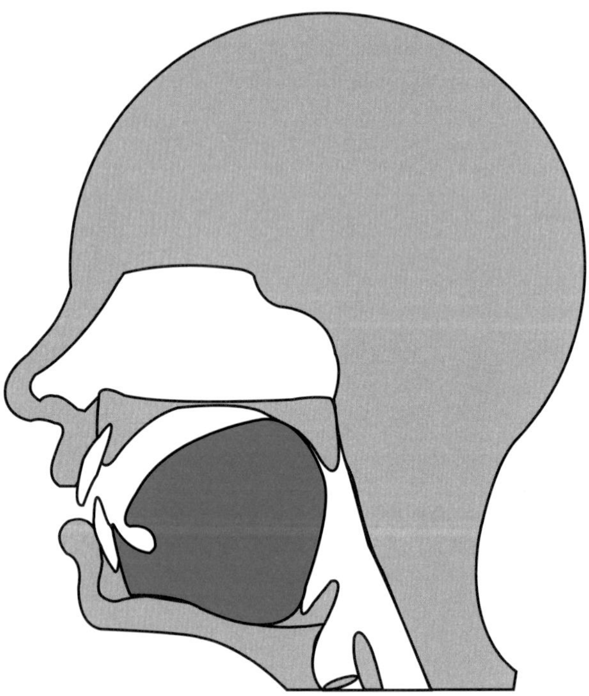

Figure 22. Position of Vocal Organs : Consonants K & G

Track 50 Sounds in Context

Listen and pay attention to how /k/ sound is pronounced in sentences.

1. Put it back in the back pack.
2. Kate ate so much cake, she had stomachache.
3. The king cooked the carrots and the queen cut the cake.

Listen and pay attention to how /g/ sound is pronounced in sentences.

1. Grandma's eggs sure looks great.
2. Glenda's guest was grinning behind the gate.
3. Gary knows how to make grapes grow bigger.

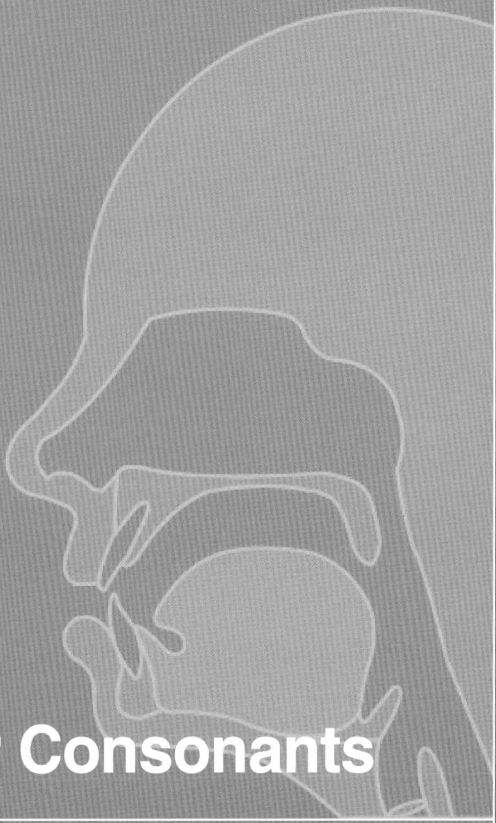

Review for Consonants

Review for Consonants

1. Dialogue for Consonant T

Track 51 **Read the following dialogue aloud and practice with a partner.**

Tricia	Do we really have to hiking, Tom? I don't feel like climbing up mountains.
Tom	Well, Why don't we go visit the ancient castle? It's about two hours away.
Tricia	Oh, right. We could take a walk around the lake instead!
Tom	I think there is a buffet at a nearby hotel as well.
Tricia	Let's look it up on the Internet. Is the computer on?
Tom	Yeah. I turned it on like twenty minutes ago.
Tricia	Cool. Can you print out the directions?
Tom	Of course. I wonder if Tanya can watch our kitten while we're gone.

2. Dialogue for Consonant L

Track 52 **Read the following dialogue aloud and practice with a partner.**

Luke	It's lunch time. Let's grab some lunch.
Lilly	I'd love to. Let's ask Laura if she's up for lunch.
Luke	Sure. But I don't know anyone named Lola.
Lilly	Laura, not Lola. You know, Laura Lee, the girl with long hair.
Luke	Oh, Laura! Is that the girl we saw at the mall the other day?
Lilly	No, that's Laurie. Laurie has short brown hair but Laura has long black hair.
Luke	Well, I guess I'll recognize her when I see her. Why don't you call and ask her?
Lilly	Right. Let me call her now and see if she feels like lunch.

3. Dialogue for Consonant RL

Track 53 **Read the following dialogue aloud and practice with a partner.**

Ralph	Grandma, can you read this story for me?
Grandma	Sure, Ralph. Let's see, it's a story about a girl who sold pearls.
Ralph	Really? I thought it was about a girl who saved the world.
Grandma	Well, this curly haired little girl apparently saves the world, too.
Ralph	Really? How does she save the world? Does she use pearls?
Grandma	Ralph, let me read the story, and you'll find out how.
Ralph	Sorry, Grandma. Please, continue. It sounds weird but interesting.
Grandma	Once upon a time, there was a girl who sold pearls at a mirror store...

4. Dialogue for Consonant th

Track 54 **Read the following dialogue aloud and practice with a partner.**

Ruth	Did you hear about the thermometer thieves on Thursday?
Matthew	You mean the three thieves who stole three thousand thermometers?
Ruth	It was actually my father's brother's friend's thermometer factory.
Matthew	Oh, that's too bad. I hope everything gets sorted out.
Ruth	I think it's going to be ok. After all, they received the three thousand thermometers in good shape.
Matthew	That's nice. The thieves must have been careful with the three thousand thin thermometers.

5. Consonants F, V, P, and B

Track 55 **Read the following dialogue aloud and practice with a partner.**

Patty	Oh, look at the peaches! They look delicious!
Frank	The fruit here looks great. Check out the pear in the back.
Patty	There is a bear in the back?
Frank	No. Not bear. Pear, you know, with a P.
Patty	Oh, pear. But there are spots on them.
Frank	How about the berries? I love strawberries and blueberries.
Patty	Ok, let's get some peaches and berries and bake pies tonight.
Frank	Sounds absolutely fantastic!

6. Consonants /s/, /z/, /ʃ/, and /ʒ/

Track 56 **Read the following dialogue aloud and practice with a partner.**

Sean	Lizzy, what are you doing on Wednesday?
Lizzy	I'm going to the zoo with Susan in the afternoon. Would you like to come?
Sean	Well, actually, I need to get a new suit, and I was wondering if you guys can help me choose something fashionable.
Lizzy	Sure. Susan and I can help you. I need to go shopping for shoes and possibly a new jacket.
Sean	Great. I knew I could count on you. Why don't I pick you guys up at the zoo around six?
Lizzy	Actually, I think four would be better. The mall gets really busy after five.
Sean	You are right. You know my car, right? It's red and it's a jeep.
Lizzy	Yes, I think so. If I don't see it, I'll give you a call.

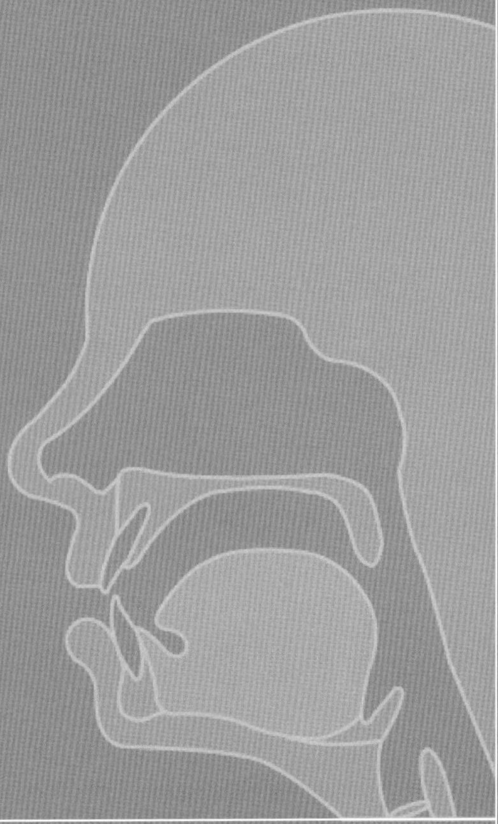

Vowels

Unit 16

Introduction to Vowels

Vowels of English

Vowels can be categorized in the following ways.

1. Vertical location of tongue: high, mid, or low
2. Horizontal location of tongue: front, middle, or back
3. Roundness of lips: round or unround
4. Tense or lax
5. Monothong or diphthong

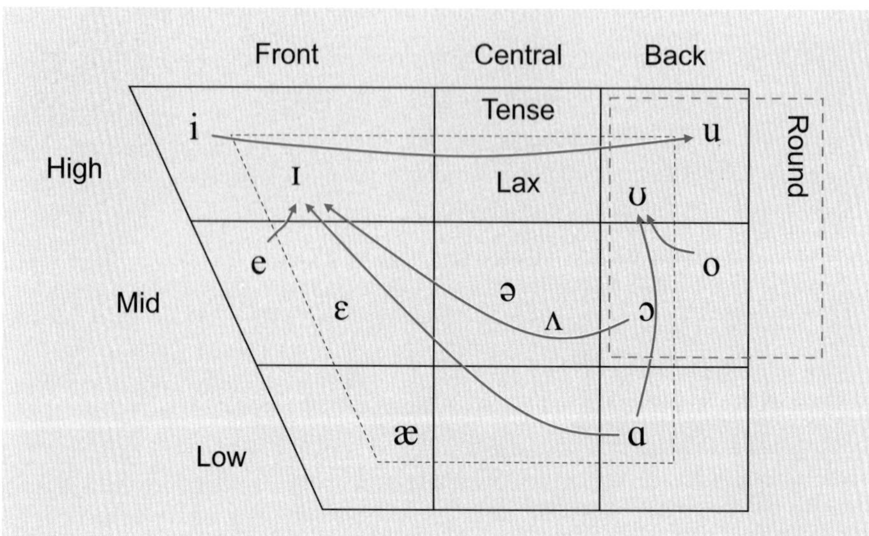

Figure 23. The Phonetic Chart of English Diphthongs, Based on Avery & Ehrlich (1992)

* There are three diphthongs in present day English.

1. /aɪ/ (i in bite)
2. /au/ (ou in house)
3. /ôɪ/ (oy in boy)

Vowel Schwa

Schwa : /ə/

How sounds are made:

mid / central / unrounded

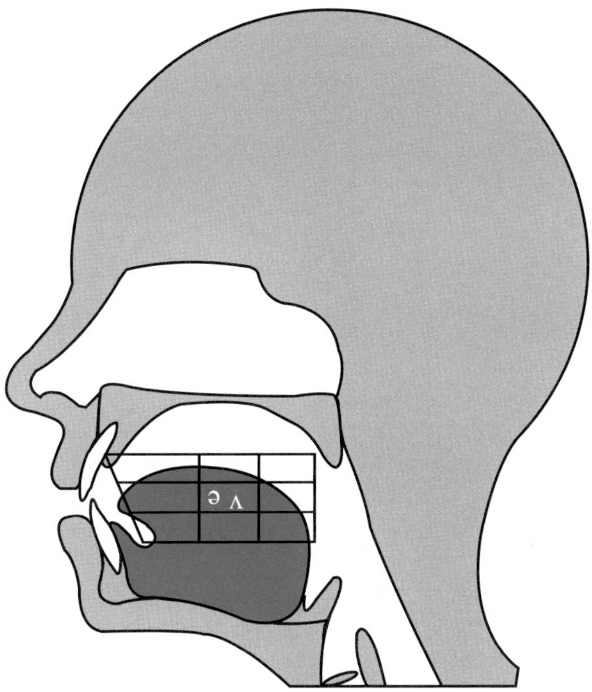

Figure 24. Position of Vocal Organs : Vowel Schwa

Track 57

Sounds in Context

Listen and pay attention to how reduced vowels are pronounced in words.

account	agree	battle	beautiful	believe
character	college	demand	destroy	different
example	family	moment	several	successful
able	incredible	general	certainty	village

Listen and pay attention to how reduced vowels are pronounced in phrases.

a cup of tea	ten to two	feel at home
wait for me	each and every	five or six
can of tuna	take it away	more than enough

Listen and pay attention to how reduced vowels are pronounced in sentences.

1. Don't forget to fasten the seat belt.
2. The tall people in the front row are blocking my sight.
3. She had a great interview at the international testing society.
4. Can you put butter and strawberry topping on my hot toast?
5. Generally, printed essays looks neater than hand written texts.

Track 58

There are general rules that can be applied to reduced vowels. Listen and pay close attention to how the vowels can become reduced depending on what comes before or after it.

1. Reduced vowels

chocolate	photography	photograph

2. Function words

cats and dogs	At ease.	I can do it.
We miss her.	Give it to him.	

3. Prefix and suffix

Inexeprience	tomorrow	advertisement
Intelligible	accomplishment	

Activity 1

Track 59

Pay attention to the vowels and practice reading the words aloud.

1	and	end	**7**	batter	better
2	Brad	bread	**8**	ladder	ladle
3	bland	blend	**9**	gas	guess
4	lather	leather	**10**	sacked	sect
5	lag	leg	**11**	bath	Beth
6	faster	fester	**12**	catch up	ketchup

Activity 2

Track 60

You will hear two sentences. Listen and check (✓) whether they sound the same or different.

#	Same	Different	Sentences
Example			*I can't talk.* *I can't talk.*
1			??? ???
2			??? ???
3			??? ???
4			??? ???
5			??? ???
6			??? ???
7			??? ???

Activity 3

Track 61

Pay close attention to reduced vowels and schwa, read the following passage aloud. Practice with the recordings.

Introducing Yourself

Hello. Nice to meet you. My name is ________ and I am a student taking a pronunciation class. I don't think my English is terrible, but I feel that having better pronunciation will help me to be a better speaker. I think it's important that people understand me the way I wanted to be understood. I also know that the way I talk can say a lot about what kind of person I am. That is why I am taking my time to learn and improve English pronunciation. I am looking forward to a great learning experience.

Unit 18

Vowel /æ/

/æ/

How sounds are made:

low/ front / unrounded

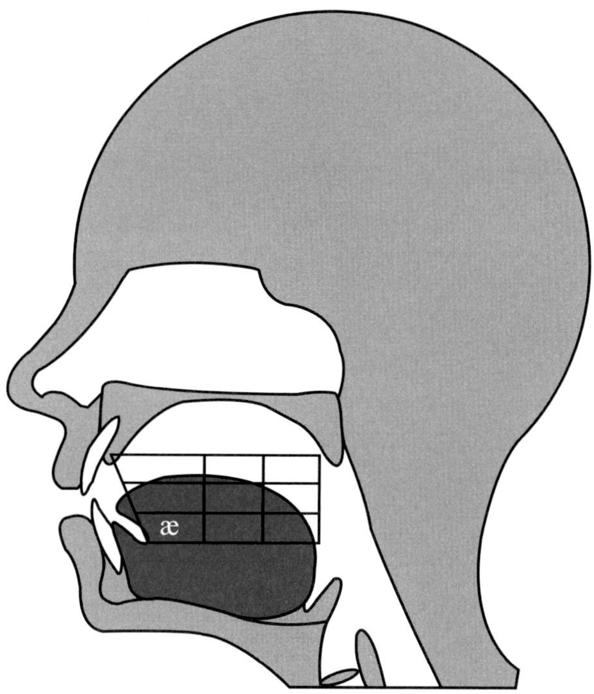

Figure 25. Position of Vocal Organs : Vowel /æ/

Track 62

Sounds in Context

Listen and pay attention to how /æ/ is pronounced in words.

at	bat	crab	dad
fat	gas	hat	Jack
lap	map	nab	pass
task	Zachary		

Listen and pay attention to how /æ/ is pronounced in sentences.

1. Pass the fat piece of bread infront of Brad.
2. My pet rabbit likeds to nap on the flannel mat.
3. The cat jumped into the bat stand.
4. Pat asked if we can head to a gas station.
5. Your task was to tally up the taxes and send faxes.

Activity 1

Track 63 **Listen and check the word you hear.**

Example	***end***	✓	***and***	
1	dead		dad	
2	head		had	
3	pled		plaid	
4	mend		manned	
5	spend		spanned	
6	bread		brad	
7	then		than	
8	ex		axe	
9	slept		slapped	
10	guest		gassed	

Activity 2

Track 64 **Listen to the recording and choose the appropriate words.**

Example: *She yelled, "(It's Kent / It's scanned / It's canned)"*

1. It is a real (bet / bed / bat), I'm not kidding.

2. The girls (sat / set / sit) the dolls down on the chair.

3. (Brad / bread / bred) was in the car across the gas station.

4. Everyone saw me walk in the room and (left / loft / laughed).

Activity 3

Track 65

Listen and fill in the blanks with the words provided in the box. Practice reading the passage aloud.

Television Tops Family Activity List, Survey Shows

Families in the US spend a ______________ 80 percent of their time together watching television, compared with 40 percent 20 years ago, according to a __________ survey by the National Families Association.

NFA had __________ in 1986 that the television would become a more popular family activity. "Our prediction came __________," NFA spokesperson Mary Johnson said. "And at this rate, television will __________ most other family activities within the next __________. Unless some other engaging __________ replaces the television, families will be spending very little time together."

The survey found that children no longer work with their parents, such as in the kitchen or in the _________, as they did in 1986. Families today spend four percent of their time together, compared with 20 percent in 1986. Families still play sports or go on __________ together, the survey showed.

spoken	whopping	decade	true
eliminate	recent	garden	spending
vacation	activity	replace	predicted

Track 66 ***Tongue Twisters***

1. The cat catchers can't catch caught cats.
2. Pretty Kitty Creighton had a cotton batten cat.
3. The cotton batten cat was bitten by a rat.
4. Can you imagine an imaginary menagerie manager imagining managing an imaginary menagerie?

Vowel /ä/

/ä/

How sounds are made:

low / back / unrounded

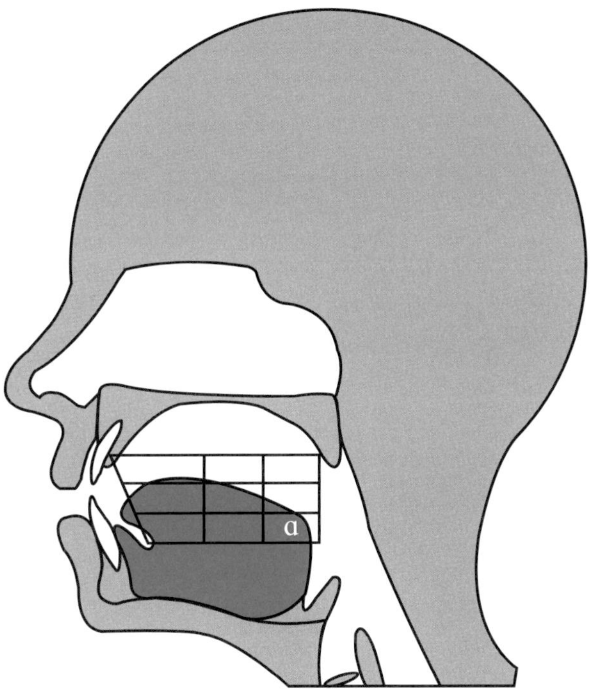

Figure 26. Position of Vocal Organs : Vowel /ä/

Track 67

Sounds in Context

Listen and pay attention to how /ä/ is pronounced in words.

bought	contrast	cot	dog
fawn	garden	hot	jock
lot	mall	not	pocket
prawn	spot	throttle	tropical

Listen and pay attention to how /æ/ is pronounced in sentences.

1. October is the season for king prawns.
2. I taught them the new song about dogs.
3. There is a coffee shop across the garden.
4. Paul is a lawyer and his mother is a law enforcement officer.
5. John, her brother, was bothering her about mowing the lawn.

Activity 1

Track 68

You will hear two words. Listen and check (✓) whether they sound the same or different.

	1	2	Same	Different
Example	*mott*	*moat*		✓
1	not	knot		
2	boat	bought		
3	odder	udder		
4	cot	caught		
5	pout	pot		
6	taut	taught		

Activity 2

Track 69

Listen and fill in the blanks with the words provided in the box. Practice reading the passage aloud.

Example: *There were nuts on the table.*

1. His _______ needed some sleep.

2. He pointed at the ______________ at the corner.

3. Dawn had ______________ supplies for the weekend.

4. Poor Bob was ______________ about the pond.

cap	knots	bought
buddy	wondering	bat
cop	body	~~nuts~~
wandering	cup	boat

Activity 3

Track 70 **Pay close attention to the vowel sound /ä/ and read the following speech aloud. Practice with the recording.**

An Excerpt from John F. Kennedy's Inaugural Address, Delivered on January 20th, 1961

In the long history of the world, only a few generations have been granted the role of defending freedom in its hour of maximum danger. I do not shrink from this responsibility -- I welcome it. I do not believe that any of us would exchange places with any other people or any other generation. The energy, the faith, the devotion which we bring to this endeavor will light our country and all who serve it. And the glow from that fire can truly light the world. And so, my fellow Americans, ask not what your country can do for you; ask what you can do for your country.

For authentic sample, go to:

http://www.americanrhetoric.com/speeches/jfkinaugural.htm

Track 71 *Tongue Twisters*

1. Ned Nott was shot and Sam Shott was not. So it is better to be Shott than Nott. Some say Nott was not shot. But Shott says he shot Nott.
2. I thought a thought. But the thought I thought wasn't the thought I thought I thought.

Further Study: Tense and Lax Vowels

Vowels are not always pronounced the way the alphabet indicates. For example, the letter A can be pronounced in several different ways. Look at the following words and pay attention to how the alphabet A is pronounced differently in each word.

Cat	/æ/	Part	/ä/	Make	/ai/
Final	/ə/	Parallel	/ɛ/	War	/o/

Tense	Lax
a	ɛ
e	i
i	ʊ (ü)
o	ə
u	ər
ä	
æ	

The vowel sounds are categorized into two categories: tense and lax vowels. Tense vowel sounds tend to form outside the dotted line, whereas lax vowels are formed inside the dotted line.

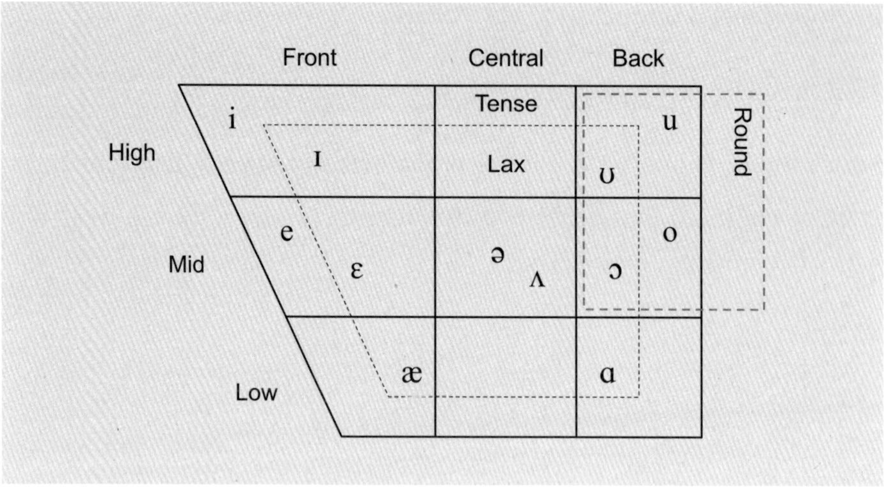

Figure 27. The Phonetic Chart of English, Based on Avery & Ehrlich (1992)

Vowels /ɪ/ & /i/

/ɪ/	/i/

How sounds are made:

high / front / unrounded

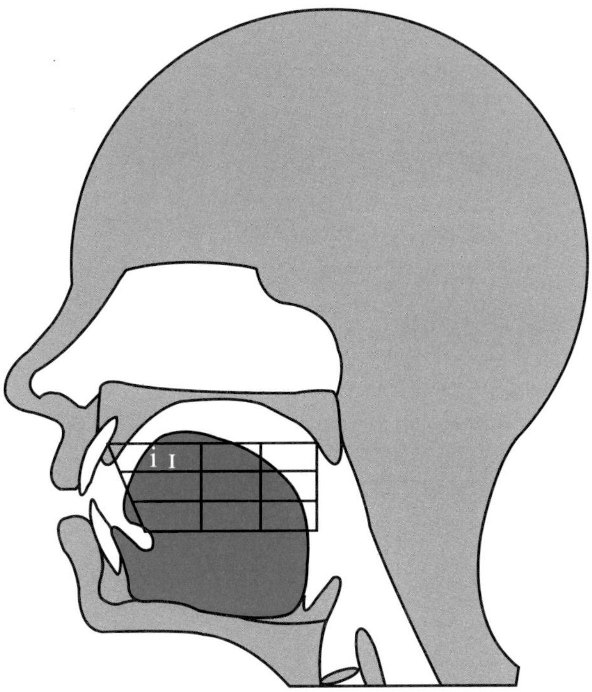

Figure 28. Position of Vocal Organs : Vowels /ɪ/ & /i/

Track 72 Sounds in Context

Listen and pay attention to how /ɪ/ and /i/ are pronounced in words.

/i/	/ɪ/	/i/	/ɪ/
bin	bean	hill	heal
breath	breathe	lick	leek
dill	deal	mid	mead
either	ether	pill	peel
fill	feel	pit	Pete
gin	Jean	sin	scene
grin	green	still	steal

Listen and pay attention to how /ɪ/ and /i/ are pronounced in words.

1. Jean has a beautiful grin.
2. I like dill salad with green bean.
3. Dogs lick their wounds to accelerate the healing process.
4. Pete had a feeling that the water was filling up too fast.
5. Be still and don't breathe too hard, I think someone is here to steal.

Activity 1

Track 73 **Listen and check (✓) the word you hear.**

	/ɪ/		/i/	
Example	*sheep*		*ship*	✓
1	heat		hit	
2	leave		live	
3	eel		ill	
4	cheap		chip	
5	seek		sick	
6	peach		pitch	

Activity 2

Track 74 **Listen and fill in the blanks. Then practice the sentences aloud.**

Example: *Look at the ship over there.*

1. I think it is time that we ________.

2. Every time I eat _______ dish, I get ____.

3. The girls are looking for a _______ farm.

4. When the ______ wave ____, air conditioner sales went up.

Activity 3

Track 75 **Pay close attention to the vowels /ɪ/ and /i/ and read the following passage aloud. Practice with the recording.**

Question: Is it better for children to grow up in the city than the country?

Children who grow up in the city may seem to have an edge over their peers in the country. They can get information faster because of efficient communications infrastructure. Interschool competitions and activities provide a variety of learning environments. City children also may have more chances to take leisure classes in music, art or sports. But children in rural area also receive quality education that is more holistic. Also they have a healthier lifestyle. They are early risers because they are not kept up at night by distracting entertainment. They breathe cleaner air. And they definitely get more exercise and more family time.

Track 76 ***Tongue Twisters***

1. These six silly sisters are sweet to meet.
2. We seek the sixth sick sheik's sixth sick sheep.
3. I slit the sheet, the sheet I slit, and on the slitted sheet I sit.
4. Picky people pick Peter Pan Peanut Butter, it's the peanut butter picky people pick.

Unit 21

Vowels /u/ & /ʊ/

/u/	/ʊ/

How sounds are made:

high / back / rounded

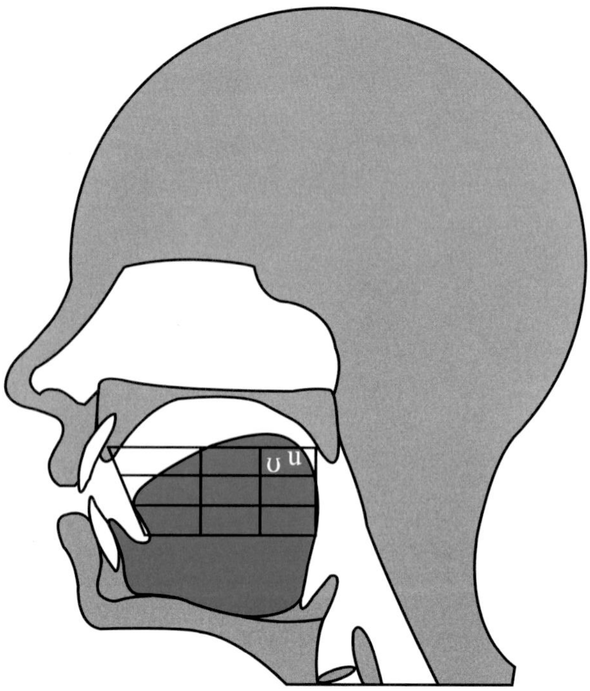

Figure 29. Position of Vocal Organs : Vowels /u/ & /ʊ/

Track 77

Sounds in Context

Listen and pay attention to how /uw/ and /ʊ/ are pronounced in words.

/u/	/ʊ/	/u/	/ʊ/
pool	pull	food	foot
tool	tull	fool	full
wool	wall	gooed	good
brood	blood	soon	soot
cooed	could	shoe	should
		two	took

Listen and pay attention to how /u/ and /ʊ/ are pronounced in words.

1. The food is on the table.
2. Should we get going soon?
3. A fool would 'pull' when it says 'push' on the door.
4. Luke doesn't like it when you look over his shoulder.
5. The new shoes are too small and my foot won't come out.

Activity 1

Track 78

Listen and check (✓) the word with different vowel than the other two words. Then practice the sentences aloud.

Example	***wool***		***would***		***world***	✓
1	full		fool		food	
2	prune		plum		flu	
3	look		Luke		fluke	
4	could		cool		rule	
5	shoot		suit		sought	
6	brood		blued		blood	

Activity 2

Track 79 **Listen and choose the word you hear and practice the sentences aloud.**

Example: *It says " pool / pull " on the door.*

1. Luke / Look, please come in and sit down.

2. That seems like black suit / soot.

3. Oh, my food / foot is cold!

4. I heard that the kid has the flute / flu.

5. Put the boot / book back where you found it.

6. The gardening tools are next to the tool / tall box.

Activity 3: Authentic Resource: Award Acceptance Speech

Track 80

Pay close attention to the vowels /u/ and /ʊ/ and read the following passage aloud. Practice with the recording.

John Nash's 1994 Nobel Prize in Economic Sciences Acceptance Address from "A Beautiful Mind (2002)"

Thank you.

I've always believed in numbers and the equations and logics that lead to reason.

But after a lifetime of such pursuits, I ask, "What truly is logic?" "Who decides reason?" My quest has taken me through the physical, the metaphysical, the delusional – and back.

And I have made the most important discovery of my career, the most important discovery of my life: It is only in the mysterious equations of love that any logic or reasons can be found.

I'm only here tonight because of you [wife, Alicia]. You are the reason I am. You are all my reasons.

Thank you.

For authentic sample, go to:

http://www.americanrhetoric.com/MovieSpeeches/moviespeechabeautifulmind.html

Track 81 ***Tongue Twisters***

1. The boot black bought the black boot back.
2. If Stu chews shoes, should Stu choose the shoes he chews?
3. A purely rural duel truly plural is better than a purely plural duel truly rural.
4. A Tudor who tooted a flute tried to tutor two tooters to toot.
   Said the two to their tutor, "Is it harder to toot or to tutor two tooters to toot?"

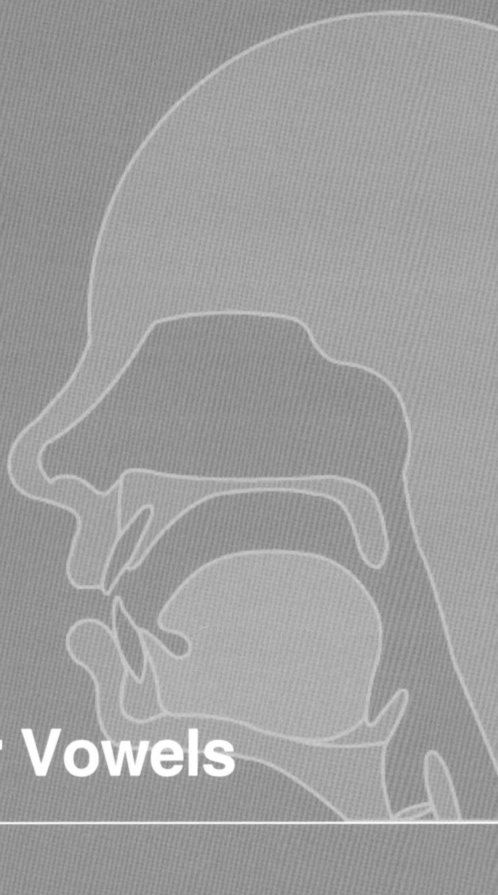

Review for Vowels

Review for Vowels

Track 82 **Read the following dialogue paying close attention to tense and lax vowels**

Jean	Hello, Pete. Come in. You look all flustered. Are you ok?
Pete	Sorry, I'm late. The traffic was really bad. But I picked up the things you asked for.
Jean	Oh, great! I hope it wasn't much trouble. Just put them on the table. Did you find everything?
Pete	No, they had black beans, ice cream, and rulers but not thumbtacks.
Jean	That's ok. I can get the tacks on my way to the pool on Saturday.
Pete	Other than the tacks, I think I got everything on the list, at least.
Jean	Well, thank you. Anyway, have a seat. Would you like some ice cream?
Pete	That'd be great. But before that, may I have something to drink?
Jean	Of course. How about peach or lemon iced tea? It's hot out, right?
Pete	Yes, it is! I need to cool off a bit. Peach sounds perfect.

Track 83 **Read the following dialogue paying close attention to reduced vowels**

Tricia	So are you going anywhere during the summer?
Kevin	I'm probably going on a family vacation to a log cabin in nearby mountain sometime in August.
Tricia	A log cabin? That sounds peaceful and refreshing. My family is planning to go to a beach. I wish we were going to the mountains.
Kevin	Why? What's wrong with the beach? The beach is always full of excitement and fun!
Tricia	Yea, exactly. You know, I prefer to relax and get plenty of sleep. I'm not exactly the hustle and bustle type.
Kevin	Oh, I love the beach. It's full of entertainment. Maybe you and I should swap our itineraries for this summer.

Review for Vowels

Track 84

Fill in the blanks with the words provided in the box and practice reading the passage aloud, paying attention to vowels in general.

Most people dress __________ for work as an act of courtesy toward their employers and clients. But some people believe that dressing smartly will impress their __________ or customers to think they are more capable. When a person is __________ according to their appearance, it is called __________. In 2002, the American news show 20/20 investigated lookism by hiring ______ _______ actors and plain-looking actors to get help with buying a car, collecting money for charity, and applying for __________. The better-looking actors were favored over the homey ones. Many think that this form of __________ can be as serious as racism, sexism and age discrimination. But some also believe that certain businesses, especially services, need __________ employees to help draw customers.

Track 85 **Pay close attention to vowels in general and read the following story.**

Snow White and the Seven Dwarves

There once was a princess named Snow White who had an evil stepmother, the queen. Every day, the queen asked her magic mirror, "Mirror, mirror on the wall, who is the fairest one of all?" and the mirror always answered "you are." But one day, the mirror answered, "Snow White." The queen was very angry. She sent her servants to have Snow White killed. But the servants felt sorry for Snow White and let her go. Snow White wandered the forest, hungry and alone, until she came to a little cabin where the seven dwarves lived. She lived happily with the seven dwarves who let her live with them.

One day, the queen asked the mirror again, "Mirror, mirror on the wall, who is the fairest one of all?" and the mirror answered, "Snow White." The queen realized that Snow White was still alive. So the queen disguised herself as a peddler and gave Snow White a poisoned apple. Snow White took a bite and fell on the floor. The dwarves were very sad and put her in a glass coffin. Then, by chance, a prince came by and saw beautiful Snow White and bent down to give her a kiss. Snow White opened her eyes and woke up. They fell in love and lived happily ever after.

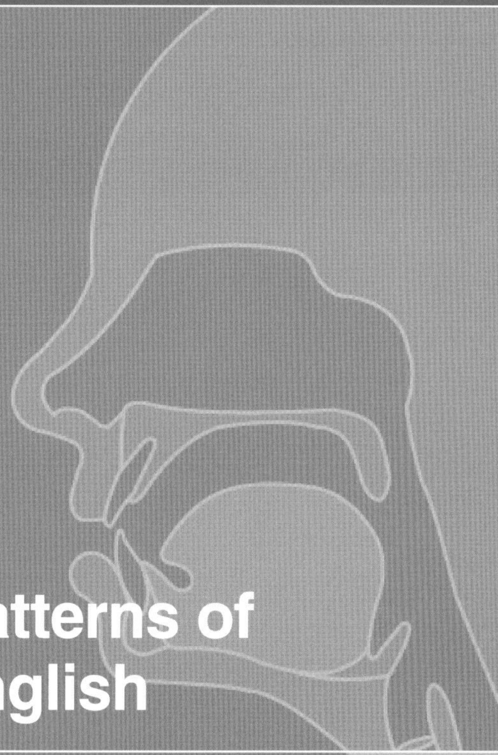

General Patterns of Spoken English

Unit 22

Letters, Numbers, Dates, & Addresses

Stress and rhythm pattern of initials, spellings and acronyms.

They are usually pronounced in groups of 3 or 4, and the last syllables are stressed.

Acronyms

Track 86 **Read the following acronyms aloud. Practice with the recording.**

SOS	USC	BMW
GPS	MBA	CIA
IBM	PGA	CSI
IMF	ROK	DMB
JFK	USA	FBI

Numbers-Teen vs. ty

Track 87

Read the following words aloud. Practice with the recording.

thirteen	thirty
fourteen	forty
fifteen	fifty
sixteen	sixty
seventeen	seventy
eighteen	eighty
nineteen	ninety

Read the following numbers aloud. Practice with the recording.

1776	1880	5015
7217	1818	3030
6116	9093	4013
1446	1330	1990

Track 88 **Read the following numbers aloud. Practice with the recording.**

Dates	
09-27-2010	September twenty seventh, two thousand ten
01-06-1986	January sixth, nineteen eighty six
May 21, 98	May twenty first, nineteen ninety eight
12/30/2003	December thirtieth, two thousand three

Track 89 **Read the following numbers aloud. Practice with the recording.**

Postal code	135-175 432-705
Phone number	02-4455-7645 042-894-6395
Mobile phone number	010-1346-7896 011-9746-5298

Activity 1

Track 90 **Listen and complete the chart.**

Name	Phone #	Email	Birthday

Activity 2

Track 91 **Read the passage aloud then put your own information in the passage.**

Hello. My name is Jung-min Park. The first name is J-U-N-G dash M-I-N, and my last name is Park, P-A-R-K. I was born in July 19th, 1989 in Daejon, and my major is biology. I'm very happy to meet you guys, and you can reach me at jmpark@email.com or 010-9764-6146. I'm looking forward to a great semester with you.

Activity 3

Track 92

Read the following dialogue aloud and practice with a partner. Substitute name, email address, and phone number with your own information.

Receptionist	Hi. Welcome to the English pronunciation workshop. May I have your name, please?
Tae Kyung	Hi. It's Tae Kyung Yoon.
Receptionist	Could you spell it for me?
Tae Kyung	Sure. The first name is two words, T-A-E, and the next word is K-Y-U-N-G. The last name is spelled Y-O-O-N.
Receptionist	Can I have your email address?
Tae Kyung	My email is tky01@email.com.
Receptionist	And phone number, please?
Tae Kyung	My number is 010-3546-6970.
Receptionist	All set! This is your name tag, and this is your lunch ticket.
Tae Kyung	Thanks.

Descriptive & Set Phrases

Descriptive Phrases

Nouns are weighted heavier than adjectives and tend to carry the weight of the new information. An adjective and a noun combination is called a descriptive phrase, and in the absence of contrast or other secondary change, the stress will fall naturally on the noun.

Set Phrases

Set phrases are cultural icons or word images and indicators of a determined use. The new meaning that the expression portrays takes over the original sense of the words, and the stress will fall on the first word.

Track 93 **Listen and practice the words with appropriate stress.**

Descriptive phrases	Set phrases
A white house	The white house
A light bulb	A light bulb
A gold fish	A goldfish
A dark room	A darkroom
A hot dog	A hotdog
A green house	A greenhouse

Activity 1

Track 94

Listen and check (✓) the appropriate box and practice the words aloud.

#	Words	Descriptive phrase	Set phrase
Example	*English teacher*		
1	black bird		
2	white house		
3	green house		
4	dark room		
5	French restaurant		
6	hot dog		

Activity 2

Track 95

Read the following dialogue aloud and practice with a partner. Substitute the underlined phrases with your personal preferences.

Waiter	Are you ready to order?
Customer	Yes, I'd like the cheeseburger combo.
Waiter	With that, you get French fries or onion rings.
Customer	I'll have the fries.
Waiter	And what would you like to drink?
Customer	Diet Coke, please.
Waiter	Will that be all?
Customer	Actually, do you have ice cream?
Waiter	Yes, we've got vanilla, chocolate, and strawberry ice cream.
Customer	I'll go with chocolate.

Unit 24

Meaningful Utterances

Some meaningless utterances can be used to show meaning when used with proper intonation.

Track 96 **Listen and practice.**

Oh, uh-uh, uh-huh, hmmm

Oh

1. Yes.
2. Really?
3. I see.

Uh-uh

1. Yes.
2. Yes?
3. I see.
4. Oh, really.

Uh-huh

1. No.
2. No way!

Hmmm

1. Let's see.
2. Interesting.
3. Hm! (whatever)
4. What?
5. I see.

Activity 1

Track 97 **Read the following dialogue aloud and practice with a partner.**

Jane	Excuse me, are you John?
John	Uh-huh.
Jane	Are you waiting for Mary?
John	Uh-huh.
Jane	Mary just asked me to tell you that she can't make it today.
John	Oh?
Jane	She got into a car accident.
John	Uh-uh!
Jane	It's a fender vender so it's not a big deal.
John	Oh.
Jane	But she says that she'll call when she gets out.
John	Uh-huh.

Activity 2

Track 98 **Read the following dialogue aloud and practice with a partner.**

Jane	Hey, do you know what the homework was for todays class.
John	Hm, that's a good question. Did you do it?
Jane	Uh-uh. I didn't even know we had homework. Did you?
John	Not yet. Let's see, what is the homework? Hm, it's...uh-oh.
Jane	Hmm? What?
John	It's a 10 page research paper!
Jane	Uh-uh!! That's impossible! We turned in 10 pages last week!
John	Hmm, you're right. Can this be right or is it a typo?
Jane	Hmm, let me ask around.

Unit 25

Filler Utterances

Filler utterances do not carry much meaning. They are usually spoken in low tone and used as throw away words. However, they are not always thrown away. For example, like is used as a filler in "the coffee was like, good." On the other hand, like is used to show mental quotation in "I was like, the coffee's good."

Like,	I mean,	you know,	it's like
kind of,	sort of,	whatever,	I was like, etc.

Activity

Read the following dialogue aloud and practice with a partner.

John	Hey, Jane. How was the test? I mean, it was really hard.
Jane	Yea. It's like, really hard. We didn't learn these, did we?
John	Well, we did. But a long time ago, you know.
Jane	Yea! We covered it like in week 1 of the class!
John	I mean, I don't think anyone is going to get an A in this class.
Jane	Whatever! Don't worry about it, it's all good, you know.
John	Come on, How can you not worry about it? It's sort of important.
Jane	I mean, it's already over, man. You can't do anything about it.
John	Well, ok. I kind of see your point. What can you do?
Jane	Right. Come on. Let's just go study for the next exam.

Thought Groups

Thought groups are read with appropriate pauses for commas, period, and question intonation to show spoken punctuations.

Activity 1

Track 100 **Read the following passage with appropriate pauses.**

It was a warm sunny day in spring I was coming home in the evening when someone said help somebody help me I turned around to see what was going on there was a lady sitting on the ground calling for help I walked up to her and asked is everything ok and she said no I fell and I can't get up I figured she had sprained her ankle so I helped her to a nearby bench called the taxi took her to the hospital and I came home.

Activity 2

Track 101 **Read the following passage with appropriate pauses.**

Yesterday I woke up ate breakfast brushed my teeth and got ready to leave the house just when I was about to leave the telephone rang and of course I picked up there was nobody on the other line so I hung up then it rang again I said hello who is this but no one answered the same thing happened over and over at least ten times I finally got fed up and called the police in the evening they told me that someones baby was playing with the phone and they told the parents to keep a better eye on their child.

Unit 27

Emphasis

The general rules of intonation are followed, but if the speaker chooses to put stress in other places, it functions to show emphasis as in underlining of important words in writing. It can also be used to show correction.

Activity 1

Track 102 **Read the following dialogue aloud and practice with a partner.**

John	Why didn't you call me last weekend?
Jane	I told you. I was working all weekend.
John	All weekend?

Activity 2

Track 103 **Read the following dialogue aloud and practice with a partner.**

John	I can't remember where I put my phone at Mikey's
Jane	You lost your phone and your keys?
John	No, I lost my phone at Mikey's!

Activity 3

Track 104 **Read the following dialogue aloud and practice with a partner.**

Jane	Where are the supplies?
John	What surprise? Is it someone's birthday?
Jane	No. Supplies for the office.
John	Oh, office supplies. They're not here yet.

Activity 4

Track 105 **Read the following dialogue aloud and practice with a partner.**

Jane	Call me at work if you need to. It's 354-5674
John	3-4-4-6-8-4?
Jane	No. 3-5-4 5-6-7-4
John	Oh, ok. I got it.

Unit 28

Added Details

The new information is stressed but not the repeated information.

*Repeated information is often omitted.

Activity 1

Track 106 **Read the following dialogue aloud and practice with a partner.**

John	I feel like a sandwich
Jane	Me, too. Tuna sandwich sounds good.

Activity 2

Track 107 **Read the following dialogue aloud and practice with a partner.**

Jane	May I have some coffee?
John	Sure.
Jane	Well, actually, coffee with cream, please.

Dialogue 3

Track 108

Read the following dialogue aloud and practice with a partner.

Jane	Are you reading Milton's Paradise Lost?
John	Yea. Have you read it?
Jane	Yes, it's a very long.
John	I believe it's more than a thousand pages long.
Jane	Isn't it like thirteen hundred pages?
John	Yea, thirteen hundred and eighty three pages to be exact.

Unit 29

Contrasting and Showing Alternatives

Stress on the items being contrasted.

When 'or' is stressed, it means the speaker doesn't have strong preference.

Activity 1

Track 109 **Read the following dialogue aloud and practice with a partner.**

Clerk	Are you paying with Visa or Mastercard?
Customer	Visa.
Clerk	Are you paying with Visa or Mastercard?
Customer	No, I'm paying with cash.

Activity 2

Track 110 **Read the following dialogue aloud and practice with a partner.**

John	Do you prefer your steak rare or well-done?
Jane	Rare or well-done, it's just meat to me.

Activity 3

Track 111 **Read the following dialogue aloud and practice with a partner.**

John	What's going on?
Jane	Not much. What are you up to?
John	I don't know. I was thinking that I need to get out.
Jane	Where are you going to go?
John	I don't know. I guess shopping or taking a walk in the park or...
Jane	Oh, talking a walk sounds good.
John	Do you want to come? How about the park or the lake?
Jane	Park or the lake, it doesn't matter. I just need some exercise.

Unit 30

Question Intonation

When checking for information, intonation tends to go up at the end. But to express opinion, intonation tends to go down. For example, 'really?' Can be used to check for information and to express opinion depending on what kind of intonation is applied.

Activity 1

Track 112 **Read the following dialogue aloud and practice with a partner.**

John	What time is it?
Jane	What time is it? It's time for you to be in class.
John	Really? Is it past 10?
Jane	Its' already 10:30! You're 30 minutes late.
John	Oh, no. I'm late? I've never been late before!

Activity 2

Track 113

Read the following dialogue aloud and practice with a partner.

John	Hey, where is your car?
Jane	Where's my car? It's in the parking lot.
John	Are you sure? I thought you parked it there, too. But... look.
Jane	Oh no! Where is my car!

Unit 31

Tag Question Intonation

For open questions, intonation goes up in tag questions.

For checking for information, it's goes down.

Activity 1

Track 114 **Read the following dialogue aloud and practice with a partner.**

Mom	John, come and sit down for a second.
John	Yes, Mom. It's not going to be long, is it?
Mom	No. I told you to clean your room yesterday, didn't I?
John	Well, I was going to do it, but I had to run to the store and...
Mom	And you haven't taken the trash out, have you?
John	I'm sorry, but the trash is picked up tomorrow, isn't it?
Mom	Oh, you're right. It's tomorrow. Can you take it out in the morning?
John	Sure, and I'll clean my room tonight.

Listening Well

It is important to show that you are listening to carry on a conversation. To show that you are listening, low tone is used. To show that you expect the speaker to continue with the story, intonation is raised.

Uh huh,	**hmm,**	**oh,**	**sure,**	**yeah, etc.**
Oh,	**I see,**	**Ok,**	**right (for instructions as well)**	

Activity 1

Track 115 **Read the following dialogue aloud and practice with a partner.**

John	I was walking home last night, and it started to rain, just a little bit.
Jane	Uh-huh.
John	But I didn't have an umbrella so I just decided to run home really fast.
Jane	Oh.
John	And thought that if I run fast enough, I won't get too wet.
Jane	Yeah.
John	But then it started to pour, like there is no tomorrow.
Jane	Really.
John	By the time I got home, I was drenched, and now I have a cold.
Jane	Oh, no.

Unit 33

Continuing a Story

A speaker tends to show that he/she is thinking by stretching or holding on to the previous word. It is used for turn keeping and buying time while carrying out a conversation.

Let's see, umm, er, or, yeah, so, ok

Activity 1

Track 116 **Read the following dialogue aloud and practice with a partner.**

Jane	Hey, John. Help me out.
John	What's the matter?
Jane	How do I get to the City Hall from here?
John	Oh, the City hall? Umm, you can take the subway or the bus.
Jane	Umm, I think I'd rather take the subway.
John	Ok. Let's see, if you get on the subway from here, it's line 3, so... umm... transfer to line 2 when you can.
Jane	Which stations are they?
John	Umm..I believe..er...just transfer to line 2 at the Seoul National University of Education. Yeah..and I think it'll take 30 minutes.
Jane	Alright. So get on the subway, transfer to line 2 at Seoul National University of Education, and er...it goes to the City hall?
John	Yes. Exactly.

Unit 34

Quoting Others

The quoted parts of the speech tend to be spoken using higher tone. It is possible to use quotation to show thoughts as well.

I said to X, and X said, X was like, X goes, etc.

Activity 1

Track 117 **Read the following dialogue aloud and practice with a partner.**

John	So are we all coming to the meeting on Wednesday at 8 a.m.?
Jane	No. Not Susan. She said that she might not be able to make it.
John	Really? She called me yesterday and said, "I'll see you on Wednesday."
Jane	I wonder why. This morning she was like, "I have to go to the airport."
John	She said to me that her mother is flying in at 7 p.m. That's probably why.
Jane	I see. She must have thought that the meeting was in the evening.
John	Wait a minute, maybe her mother is arriving in the morning.
Jane	Oh, I don't know. We should just call her ask her to be sure.
John	But she said, "don't call me unless it's an emergency!"
Jane	Oh, great. Let me send her a text message first.

Unit 35

Humor

Skewed intonation can be used to show humor and sarcasm.

Stresses are placed on unusual syllables that do not follow the regular pattern.

Activity 1

Track 118 **Read the following dialogue aloud and practice with a partner.**

Sarah	Hello.
Andy	Hi, Sarah, This is Andy.
Sarah	Hey, did you get to LA ok?
Andy	No. I'm actually stuck in Hawaii.
Sarah	What? What happened?
Andy	There was some weather problem so we landed in Honolulu.
Sarah	Oh, lucky you. Did the airline put you in a hotel?
Andy	Yeah, I'm staying at a five star hotel, but the weather is too nice.
Sarah	Oh, how terrible. That must be a real pain.
Andy	Hahaha, yeah. And the beach is only a block away.

Depending on the Context

Depending on the context of who, when, where, why, intonation pattern may change drastically.

Activity 1

Track 119

Read the following dialogue aloud and practice with a partner.

John	Hey, What's up?
Jane	Oh, hi. How have you been?
John	Just fine. How about you?
Jane	Everything is all good.
John	Well, that's great.
Jane	Yeah, look, I'm sorry but I have to go.
John	Sure, we'll catch up later. Take care.
Jane	Right. Give me a call, ok? Bye.

Dialogue in context

Track 120

Read the dialogue according to the context given below and practice with a partner.

#	Role	Place
1	Friends who have not seen each other since elementary school	On college campus
2	Two international spies meeting to exchange important information	At night, in a dark street corner
3	Two boxers who plan to fight in a match in 2 days.	At the gym
4	Two old people who can't hear very well	On the street
5	*Your choice.*	*Your choice.*

Unit 37

Polite Alternatives

It is important to remember that informal is not necessarily casual, and casual does not mean rude. You can be polite and informal at the same time.

Formal usage means that there are certain required structures that need to be followed. Formal language is used most often in the court of law, international conferences, etc.

Casual vs. Polite

Informal vs. Formal

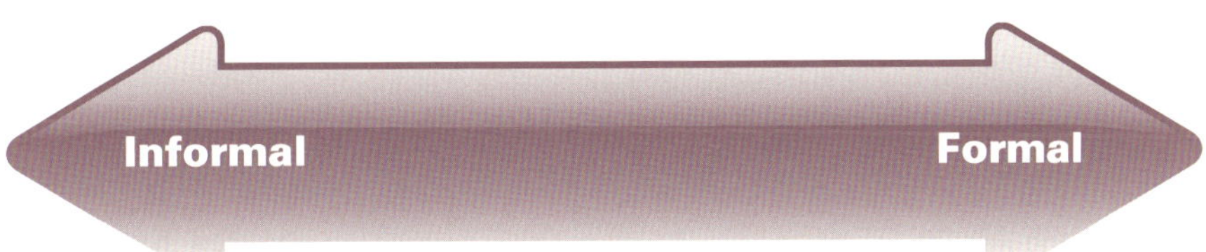

Dialogue in context

Track 121 **Listen to the recording, and practice them aloud.**

	Casual	Polite
1	What do you want?	Want can I do for you? What would you like?
2	I don't care.	Whatever you like.
3	Whatever.	It doesn't matter.
4	I want a coke.	I'd like a coke.
5	Give me a coke.	May I have some Coke?
6	What's your name?	Can I have you name?
7	No.	That's ok. / Maybe later.
8	What?	Sorry? / Pardon?

Activity 1

Track 122 **Read the following dialogue aloud and practice with a partner.**

John	What do you want?
Jane	Whatever. I don't care.
John	Come on. What about milk?
Jane	Hmmm. No. I want Coca-Cola.
John	What?
Jane	Coke.
John	Oh, Coke. Just a second.

Activity 2

Track 123 **Change the dialogue using the polite expressions and practice with a partner.**

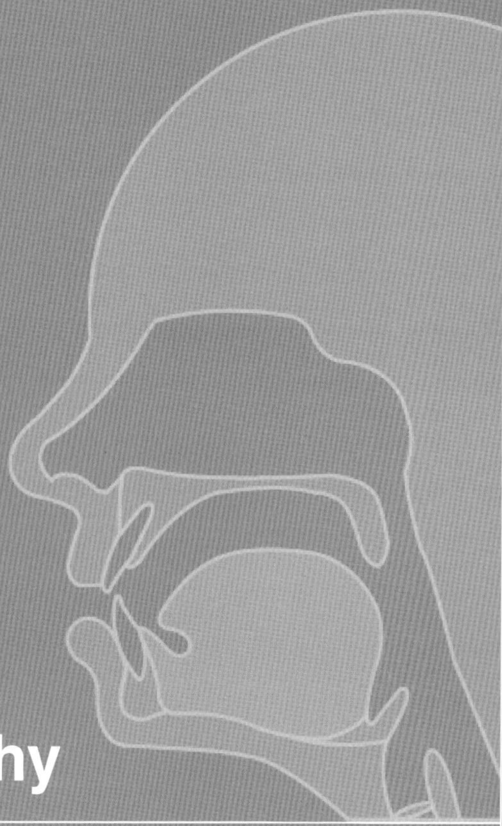

Bibliography

Bibliography

Avery, P., & Ehrlich, S. (1992). *Teaching American English Pronunciation.* Oxford: Oxford University Press.

Denes, P.B., & Pinson, E. N. (1963). *The Speech Chain.* New Jersey: Bell Telephone laboratories.

Ladefoged, P. (2006). *A course in phonetics (5th ed.)* Boston: Thomson Wadsworth.

Lee, H. B. (2002). *Dictionary of Korean Pronunciation.* Seoul National University Press, Seoul.

The International Phonetic Association (2005). *The International Phonetic Alphabet.* Retrieved March 15, 2010, from the World Wide Web: http://www.langsci.ucl.ac.uk/ipa/

Yoon, S. Y. (2011). *The impact of blenden learning on the development of English spoken skills at university level.* Unpublished doctoral dissertaion. Hankuk University of Foreign Studies, Seoul, Korea.

Yoon, S. Y., & Lee, C. H. (2011). A study on voice recording and feedback through BBS in teaching and lerning pronunciation. *Multimedia-Assisted Language Learning, 12*(2), 189-218.

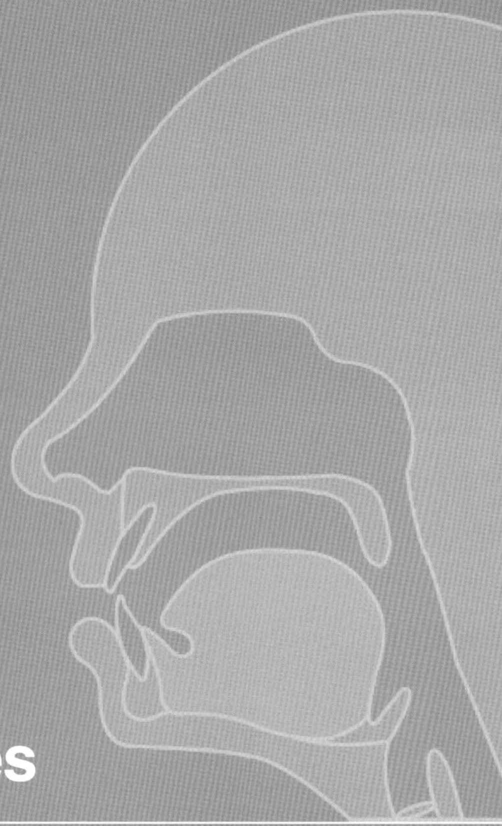

Appendices

Useful websites

http://www.uiowa.edu/~acadtech/phonetics/english/frameset.html

How sounds are made

http://fonetiks.org/

English accents

http://www.pronuncian.com/Default.aspx

Introduction to English pronunciation

http://www.e-pron.com/

Stress and intonation

http://www.soundsofenglish.org/

Pronouncing English sounds (minimal pairs) and word stress

http://www.englishclub.com/pronunciation/word-stress.htm

Word stress rules

http://www.englishclub.com/pronunciation/sentence-stress.htm

Sentence stress rules

http://www-personal.umich.edu/%7Ecellis/heteronym.html

Heteronym (same spelling, different sound)

http://esl.about.com/library/listening/accents/blaccents.htm?once=true&

Regional accent listening gallery

http://accent.gmu.edu/browse.php

Accent by countries

http://international.ouc.bc.ca/pronunciation/

Minimal pairs, dictation, worksheets, video clips, etc for segmentals

http://www.manythings.org/pp/ (http://www.manythings.org/)

Minimal pair practice

http://www.lclark.edu/~krauss/toppicks/pronunciation.html

Pronunciation by levels

http://pauillac.inria.fr/~xleroy/stuff/english-pronunciation.html

Pronunciation test-a poem composed of words with pronunciation difficulties

http://www.esl-lab.com/

Listening by levels and purpose

Consonants

Unit 7 Consonants T & D

Activity 1

	Words	Beginning	Middle	Ending
Example	*eastern*		✓	
1	topic	✓		
2	arctic		✓	
3	foster		✓	
4	cast			✓
5	temporary	✓		
6	crystal		✓	
7	accurate			✓
8	timid	✓		
9	multiply		✓	
10	create			✓

Activity 2

1. Endinging T

It is really not quite right to light night-lights with their slight lights on a light night like tonight.

2. Unstressed T before N

Pretty Kitty Creighton had a cotton batten cat.

The cotton batten cat was bitten by a rat.

3. Middle T and Unstressed T

Betty Botter had some butter, "But," she said, "this butter's bitter.

If I bake this bitter butter, it would make my batter bitter."

4. Intonation with D

If you understand, say "understand."

If you don't understand, say "don't understand."

But if you understand and say "don't understand."

How do I understand that you understand. Understand!?

5. T Combination

A. Did you see the little kitten print satin curtain?

B. Don't eat in front of the computer while surfing the Internet.

C. A celebrity is giving a talk at the Intercontinental hotel.

D. I'd like to visit the castle on Saturday and take a walk in the garden.

E. He passed the computerized test but failed to do well on the interview.

Answer key

Activity 3

Introducing yourself

Hello. Nice to meet you. My name is Peter and I am a student taking a pronunciation class. I don't think my English is terrible, but I feel that having better pronunciation will help me in becoming a better speaker. I think it's important that I get understood the way I wanted to be. Also the way I talk tells people what kind of person I am. That is why I am taking my time to learn and improve my English pronunciation. I am looking forward to a great learning experience.

T= underline

Further study 2: -ed endinds

Activity 1

	Verbs	-d	-t	-id
Example	*crossed*		✓	
1	hated			✓
2	watched		✓	
3	yelled	✓		
4	invited			✓
5	worked		✓	
6	married	✓		
7	saved	✓		
8	folded			✓
9	created			✓
10	learned	✓		
11	touched		✓	
12	rocked		✓	

Answer key

Activity 2

Example: *She looked refreshed when she walked out of the spa.*

(d / [t] / id) *(d / [t] / id)*

1. The dog reached the corner, turned left and ran away.

(d / [t] / id) ([d] / t / id)

2. The boy yelled at his classmate who cheated on the test.

([d] / t / id) (d / t / [id])

3. After I invited them to dinner, I vacuumed and cleaned the house.

(d / t / [id]) ([d] / t / id) ([d] / t / id)

4. He folded the laundry while she washed the dishes, wiped the counter.

([d] / t / id) (d / [t] / id) (d / [t] / id)

Unit 8 Consonant L

Activity 1. 2

Example:	*plumb*	*palm*	*plunder*	*plump*
1.	shoal	shoulder	should	shelf
2.	clam	calm	calamity	calcium
3.	almond	alarmed	allergy	allotted
4.	salamander	salient	supply	salmon
5.	follow	fold	folk	file

Answer key

Activity 2

Example: *The lovely rose is (glowing / growing).*

1. Your answer is (wrong / long).

2. On Sundays, I take time out to (pray / play).

3. It seems as if she is (boring / bowling).

4. Why don't we (work / walk) for about an hour before dinner.

5. His dream is to become a (pirate / pilot).

6. Be careful not to walk on the (grass / glass).

Activity 3

I took a walk in the park. It was very cold and I was wearing the right clothes. On the road, I found a lock. I realized that it was long. I didn't want an extra load so I didn't pick it up. I continued to work on my stroll. When I came to a rock, I decided to add it to my collection. By the time I came home, it was not light anymore but I was barely tired.

Unit 9 Consonant R

Activity 1

Example	*Tower*		*Towel*	✓
1	file		fire	✓
2	heel	✓	hear	
3	teal		tear	✓
4	peer		peel	✓
5	right	✓	light	
6	lead	✓	read	

Answer key

Activity 2-Minimal Pair

Example: *He is an avid (reader / leader).*

1. (Law / Raw) is there to be kept, not broken.

2. The (climb / crime) was not only terrifying but tiring.

3. When the tall player threw the ball, it hit the (limb / rim) and went in.

4. One problem with bringing in stray animals is that they might have (fleas / freeze).

5. Did you see how much Arnold's (belly / berry) has grown over the summer?

Activity 3

Little Red Riding Hood

A **l**ong, **l**ong time ago, a gir**l** ca**ll**ed **L**itt**l**e Red Riding Hood went to visit her grandmother. Whi**l**e Litt**l**e Red Riding Hood stro**ll**ed a**l**ong the **l**ove**l**y country road, the big bad wo**l**f came and swa**ll**owed Granny. Then he put on Granny's cap, got into Granny's bed, and covered up with b**l**ankets. **L**itt**l**e Red Riding Hood arrived and said, "Granny, what big ears you have!" and the wo**l**f rep**l**ied, "**All** the better to hear you with, my dear!" Then she said, "Granny, what big eyes you have!" and the wo**l**f rep**l**ied, "**All** the better to see you with, my dear!" Then **L**itt**l**e Red Riding Hood said, "Granny, what big teeth you have!" and the wo**l**f rep**l**ied, "**All** the better to eat you with, my dear!" Then the wo**l**f swa**ll**owed up the gir**l**. **L**ucki**l**y, a passing by **l**umberjack saw it a**ll**. He batt**l**ed the wo**l**f and rescued **L**itt**l**e Red Riding Hood and Granny. **L**ater, three of them drank **l**emonade together and **l**ived happi**l**y ever after.

L=bold

R=underline

Answer key

Unit 10 Consonant TH

Activity 1

Example	***Same***		***Different***	✓	***sought/thought***
1	Same		Different	✓	*bread/breathe*
2	Same	✓	Different		*dose/dose*
3	Same		Different	✓	*either/ether*
4	Same		Different	✓	*ladder/rather*
5	Same	✓	Different		*other/other*
6	Same	✓	Different		*they/they*

Activity 2

Example: *Either you are with us or you are with them.*

1. That man is healthy, wealthy, and well-educated.

2. I need to take the temperature, but I can't find the thermometer.

3. Take the thirty little sweaters to the thrift store mother showed you on Thursday.

4. They all thought that they were utterly lost until those hikers showed up in their path.

5. These moths tend to be active at night, but some in southern hemisphere thrive in the day time, too.

Activity 3

Please call Stella. Ask her to bring these things with her from the store: Six spoons of fresh snow peas, five thick slabs of blue cheese, and maybe a snack for her brother Bob. We also need a small plastic snake and a big toy frog for the kids. She can scoop these things into three red bags, and we will go meet her Wednesday at the train station.

th=underline

Answer key

Unit 11 Consonants F & V

Activity 1

Example	often		oven	✓	open	
1	fan		fran		pan	✓
2	ferry	✓	very		fairy	
3	half		halve	✓	help	
4	pew	✓	few		view	
5	ripe		life		live	✓
6	save		self	✓	safe	

Activity 2

Example: *The <u>view</u> from the window is quite nice.*

1. Would you like a <u>half</u> or a quarter of this apple?

2. Cover your mouth when you <u>cough</u>, especially if you are sick.

3. When you <u>leave</u>, please turn <u>off</u> the computers and the lights.

4. It is recommended that you exercise <u>often</u>, at least three times a week.

5. The youth <u>offered</u> his seat to an elderly lady who was carrying a <u>heavy</u> load.

~~leave~~	few	happy	laugh
live	~~cough~~	~~view~~	~~often~~
of	~~offered~~	calf	~~half~~
~~heavy~~	free	~~off~~	self

Answer key

Activity 3

Frank and his wife, Olivia, flew to Florida for vacation. They had lots delicacies made from fish and tropical fruits. When they got back home to Nevada, they couldn't fit into their old clothes anymore. They've gained fifteen kilograms over two weeks. They were horrified. Frank felt fat and Olivia thought she suffered from obesity at first. But soon, they decided that since they had such a fantastic time that they decided to brighten up and go shopping for new clothes instead.

Unit 12 Consonants P & B

Activity 1

Example	***pray***	***pray***	***fray***
1	face	face	pace
2	bee	pea	bee
3	shift	shipped	shipped
4	pane	feign	pane
5	coffee	copy	copy
6	cheap	cheap	chief

Activity 2

Example: *There is a (bear / pear) in the large tree.*

1. Can you get the pen from the (back / pack)?

2. This (beach / peach) is great. I love it.

3. Let's get a (cap / cab) for the baseball game.

4. I heard that (they've earned / they burned) the diploma last semester.

Answer key

Activity 3

Weather Forecast

Good evening and welcome to the Wednesday's weather report. Well, we're going to have mixed weather across the country. The cold front that's been moving north may bring snow in the u**pp**er region tomorrow. There's a strong chance the snow will continue until Friday.

Another cold front is moving south-west and should arrive on the west coast tomorrow evening. We can ex**p**ect cold winds and rain late Friday afternoon. It's **p**ossible that this rain will continue overnight, until Saturday.

On the east coast, we are ex**p**ecting a slight rise in tem**p**eratures, from today's high of seven degrees to high as fifteen degrees. But the mild weather won't last very long. The cold front affecting the rest of the country will reach the east by Sunday evening.

P= bold

B= underline

Unit 13 Consonants S & Z

Activity 1

Example: *zip*

1. prices
2. raising
3. knees
4. peace
5. Zack
6. Sue
7. Jane
8. zip

Activity 2

1. If you don't take the advice I give you, I can't advise you.

2. The coffee shop close to my house closes early.

3. The price you have to pay is worth the prize.

4. I don't know for sure but I think Sue is at the zoo.

5. Your button is loose, you might lose it if it falls off.

Activity 3

An Excerpt from Gettysburg Address by Abraham Lincoln

But, in a larger **s**en**s**e, we cannot dedicate, we cannot con**s**ecrate, we cannot hallow thi**s** ground. The brave men, living and dead who **s**truggled here have con**s**ecrated it far above our poor power to add or detract. The world will little note nor long remember what we **s**ay here, but it can never forget what they did here. It is for u**s** the living rather to be dedicated here to the unfinished work which they who fought here have thu**s** far **s**o nobly advan**c**ed. It is rather for u**s** to be here dedicated to the great ta**s**k remaining before u**s** – that from these honored dead we take increased devotion to that cause for which they gave the la**s**t full measure of devotion – that we here highly resolve that these dead shall not have died in vain, that thi**s** nation under God shall have a new birth of freedom, and that government of the people, by the people, for the people shall not perish from the earth.

/s/= bold
/z/= underline

Further study –s endings

Activity 1

	Verbs	-z	-s	-iz
Example	***gasses***			✓
1	clocks		✓	
2	pencils	✓		
3	classes			✓
4	balloons	✓		
5	sheets		✓	
6	pickles	✓		
7	purses			✓
8	ships		✓	
9	units		✓	
10	axes			✓
11	checks		✓	
12	bags	✓		
13	scissors	✓		
14	students		✓	

Answer key

Activity 2

Example : *Jenny's brothers all wear blue jeans.*

1. She never watches horror movies without her dogs.

   (s / z / [iz])   (s / [z] / iz)   (s / [z] / iz)

2. There are axes in her trunk as well as spikes and screws.

   (s / z / [iz])   ([s] / z / iz) (s / [z] / iz)

3. The students like the chapter on plants and animals.

   ([s] / z / iz)   ([s] / z / iz) (s / [z] / iz)

4. He examines the sights carefully, including the exits and entrances.

   ([s] / z / iz)   ([s] / z / iz) ([s] / z / iz)

Unit 19 Consonants /ʃ/ & /ʒ/

Activity 1

	/s/		/ʃ/	
Example	*Sue*	✓	*shoe*	
1	Sam		sham	✓
2	sop	✓	shop	
3	sear	✓	shear	
4	rust		rushed	✓
5	lease		leash	✓

Activity 2

Example: *(Seizures / Scissors) are dangerous at times.*

1. We saw a dog (watching / washing) cars.

2. They were planning to (chew / shoe / sue) him.

3. I saw a (batch / badge / bash)on my neighbor's yard.

4. He was (leasing / leashing / leaching) the dog when she walked in the door.

Answer key

Activity 3

My Hobby

My hobby is going to the **sh**opping mall. I used to go fi**sh**ing at the sea**sh**ore on the weekend, but now I spend time at the **sh**opping mall. I'm not rich, so I have to choose carefully when I charge my credit card. Last weekend, I went to the **sh**opping center with my cousin, George, from Virginia. We bought matching **sh**irts. Then we watched a movie about Trojan soldiers and went for desserts. We had a good time, and I envision an even more pleasurable **sh**opping experience when the sales begin next month.

/ʃ/= bold
/ʒ/= underline

Review for consonants

1. Dialogue for Consonant T

Tricia	Do we really have to hiking, Tom? I don't feel like climbing up mountains.
Tom	Well, Why don't we go visit the ancient castle? It's about two hours away.
Tricia	Oh, right. We could take a walk around the lake instead!
Tom	I think there is a buffet at a nearby hotel as well.
Tricia	Let's look it up on the Internet. Is the computer on?
Tom	Yeah. I turned it on like twenty minutes ago.
Tricia	Cool. Can you print out the directions?
Tom	Of course. I wonder if Tanya can watch our kitten while we're gone.

T= underline

Answer key

2. Dialogue for Consonant L

Luke	It's lunch time. Let's grab some lunch.
Lilly	I'd love to. Let's ask Laura if she's up for lunch.
Luke	Sure. But I don't know anyone named Lola.
Lilly	Laura, not Lola. You know, Laura Lee, the girl with long hair.
Luke	Oh, Laura! Is that the girl we saw at the mall the other day?
Lilly	No, that's Laurie. Laurie has short brown hair but Laura has long black hair.
Luke	Well, I guess I'll recognize her when I see her. Why don't you call and ask her?
Lilly	Right. Let me call her now and see if she feels like lunch.

L= underline

3. Dialogue for Consonant RL

Ralph	Grandma, can you read this story for me?
Grandma	Sure, Ralph. Let's see, it's a story about a girl who sold pearls.
Ralph	Really? I thought it was about a girl who saved the world.
Grandma	Well, this curly haired little girl apparently saves the world, too.
Ralph	Really? How does she save the world? Does she use pearls?
Grandma	Ralph, let me read the story, and you'll find out how.
Ralph	Sorry, Grandma. Please, continue. It sounds weird but interesting.
Grandma	Once upon a time, there was a girl who sold pearls at a mirror store...

RL= underline

4. Dialogue for Consonant th

Ruth	Did you hear about the thermometer thieves on Thursday?
Matthew	You mean the three thieves who stole three thousand thermometers?
Ruth	It was actually my father's brother's friend's thermometer factory.
Matthew	Oh, that's too bad. I hope everything gets sorted out.
Ruth	I think it's going to be ok. After all, they received the three thousand thermometers in good shape.
Matthew	That's nice. The thieves must have been careful with the three thousand thin thermometers.

TH= underline

5. Consonants F, V, P, and B

Patty	Oh, look at the peaches! They look delicious!
Frank	The fruit here looks great. Check out the pear in the back.
Patty	There is a bear in the back?
Frank	No. Not bear. Pear, you know, with a P.
Patty	Oh, pear. But there are spots on them.
Frank	How about the berries? I love strawberries and blueberries.
Patty	Ok, let's get some peaches and berries and bake pies tonight.
Frank	Sounds absolutely fantastic!

F, V, P, and B= underline

6. Consonants /s/, /z/, /ʃ/, and /ʒ/

Sean	Lizzy, what are you doing on Wednesday?
Lizzy	I'm going to the zoo with Susan in the afternoon. Would you like to come?
Sean	Well, actually, I need to get a new suit, and I was wondering if you guys can help me choose something fashionable.
Lizzy	Sure. Susan and I can help you. I need to go shopping for shoes and possibly a new jacket.
Sean	Great. I knew I could count on you. Why don't I pick you guys up at the zoo around six?
Lizzy	Actually, I think four would be better. The mall gets really busy after five.
Sean	You are right. You know my car, right? It's red and it's a jeep.
Lizzy	Yes, I think so. If I don't see it, I'll give you a call.

/s/, /z/, /ʃ/, and /ʒ/= underline

Answer key

Vowels

Unit 17 Vowel schwa

Sounds in Context

Words

Account	Agree	Battle	Beautiful	Believe
Character	College	Demand	Destroy	Different
Example	Family	Moment	Several	Successful
Able	Incredible	General	Certainty	Village

Phrases

A cup of tea

Feel at home

Each and every

Can of tuna

More than enough

Ten to two

Wait for me

Five or six

Take it away

Sentences

We can stay or we can go home.

I don't know, but I can ask him to give examples.

The characters in the musical seemed quite different from the book.

You need to be able to remember the direction to her apartment.

Reduced vowels=underlined

Activity 2

#	Same	Different	Sentences
Example		✓	*I can't talk.* *I can't talk.*
1		✓	I saw each and every time. I saw each one every time.
2	✓		It's two to six. It's two to six.
3		✓	It's two-two-six. It's two till six.
4	✓		Get sound sleep. Get sound sleep.
5		✓	Get some sleep. Get sound sleep.
6		✓	Take a box of them. Take a box off them.
7	✓		Make sure today is the day. Make sure today is the day.

Activity 3

Hello. Nice to meet you. My name is ______ and I am u student taking a pronunciation class. I don't think my English is terrible, but I feel that having better pronunciation will help me to be a better speaker. I think it's important that people understand me the way I wanted to be understood. I also know that the way I talk can say a lot about what kind of person I am. That is why I am taking my time to learn and improve English pronunciation. I am looking forward to a great learning experience.

Suggested reduction=underline

Note that depending on the reader, vowels may get more or less reduced.

Answer key

Unit 18 Vowel /æ/

Sounds in Context

Sentences

Pass the fat piece of bread infront of Brad.

My pet rabbit likes to nap on the flannel mat.

The cat jumped into the bat stand.

Pat asked if we can head to a gas station.

Your task was to tally up the taxes and send faxes.

/æ/= underline

Activity 1

Example	*end*	✓	*and*	
1	dead	✓	dad	
2	head		had	✓
3	pled		plaid	✓
4	mend	✓	manned	
5	spend		spanned	✓
6	bread	✓	Brad	
7	then	✓	than	
8	ex		axe	✓
9	slept		slapped	✓
10	guest	✓	gassed	

Activity 2

Example: *She yelled, " (It's Kent / It's scanned / It's canned)."*

1. It is a real (bet / bed / bat), I'm not kidding.

2. The girls (sat / set / sit) the dolls down on the chair.

3. (Brad / bread / bred) was in the car across the gas station.

4. Everyone saw me walk in the room and (left / loft / laughed).

Activity 3

Television Tops Family Activity List, Survey Shows

Families in the US spend a whopping 80 percent of their time together watching television, compared with 40 percent 20 years ago, according to a recent survey by the National Families Association.

NFA had predicted in 1986 that the television would become a more popular family activity. "Our prediction came true," NFA spokesperson Mary Johnson said. "And at this rate, television will eliminate most other family activities within the next decade. Unless some other engaging activity replaces the television, families will be spending very little time together."

The survey found that children no longer work with their parents, such as in the kitchen or in the garden, as they did in 1986. Families today spend four percent of their time together, compared with 20 percent in 1986. Families still play sports or go on vacation together, the survey showed.

Unit 19 /ä/

Sounds in Context

Sentences

October is the season for king prawns.

I taught them the new song about dogs.

There is a coffee shop across the garden.

Paul is a lawyer and his mother is a law enforcement officer.

John, her brother, was bothering her about mowing the lawn.

Activity 1

	1	2	Same	Different
Example	*mott*	*moat*		✓
1	not	knot	✓	
2	boat	bought		✓
3	odder	udder		✓
4	cot	caught	✓	
5	pout	pot		✓
6	taut	taught	✓	

Answer key

Activity 2

Example: *There were nuts on the table.*

1. His body needed some sleep.

2. He pointed at the cop at the corner.

3. Dawn had bought supplies for the weekend.

4. Poor Bob was wandering about the pond.

cap	knots	bought
buddy	wondering	bat
cop	body	~~nuts~~
wandering	cup	boat

Activity 3

An Excerpt from John F. Kennedy's Inaugural Address, Delivered on January 20th, 1961,

In the long history of the world, only a few generations have been granted the role of defending freedom in its hour of maximum danger. I do not shrink from this responsibility -- I welcome it. I do not believe that any of us would exchange places with any other people or any other generation. The energy, the faith, the devotion which we bring to this endeavor will light our country and all who serve it. And the glow from that fire can truly light the world.

And so, my fellow Americans, ask not what your country can do for you; ask what you can do for your country.

/ä/=underlined

Note that depending on readers, /ä/ may become reduced.

Answer key

Unit 20 Vowels /ɪ/ & /i/

Sounds in Context

Sentences

Jean has a beautiful gr**i**n.

I like d**i**ll salad with green bean.

Dogs l**i**ck their wounds to accelerate the healing process.

Pete had a feeling that the water was f**i**lling up too fast.

Be st**i**ll and don't breathe too hard, I think someone is here to steal.

/i/=**bold**
/ɪ/=underline

Activity 1

	/ɪ/		/i/	
Example	*sheep*		*ship*	✓
1	heat	✓	hit	
2	leave		live	✓
3	eel	✓	ill	
4	cheap	✓	chip	
5	seek		sick	✓
6	peach		pitch	✓

Activity 2

Example: *Look at the ship over there.*

1. I think it is time that we leave.

2. Every time I eat eel dish, I get ill.

3. The girls are looking for a peach farm.

4. When the heat wave hit, air conditioner sales went up.

Answer key

Activity 3

Question: Is it better for children to grow up in the city than the country?

Children who grow up in the city may seem to have an edge over their peers in the country. They can get information faster because of efficient communications infrastructure. Interschool competitions and activities provide a variety of learning environments. City children also may have more chances to take l**ei**sure classes in music, art or sports. But children in rural area also rec**ei**ve quality education that is more holistic. Also they have a healthier lifestyle. They are early risers because they are not kept up at night by distracting entertainment. They breathe cl**ea**ner air. And they definitely get more exercise and more family time.

/ɪ/=**bold**
/i/=underline
Note that depending on readers, /i/ may become reduced.

Unit 21 Vowels /u/ vs. /ʊ/

Sounds in Context

Sentences

The food is on the table.

Sh**ou**ld we get going soon?

A fool w**ou**ld 'p**u**ll' when it says 'p**u**sh' on the door.

Luke doesn't like it when you l**oo**k over his shoulder.

The new shoes are too small and my f**oo**t won't come out.

/ʊ/=bold
/u/=underline

Activity 1

Example	*wool*		*would*		*world*	✓
1	full		fool	✓	food	
2	prune		plum	✓	flu	
3	look	✓	Luke		fluke	
4	could	✓	cool		rule	
5	shoot		suit		sought	✓
6	brood		blued		blood	✓

Answer key

Activity 2

Example: *It says " pool / pull " on the door.*

1. Luke / Look, please come in and sit down.

2. That seems like black suit / soot.

3. Oh, my food / foot is cold!

4. I heard that the kid has the flute / flu.

5. Put the boot / book back where you find it.

6. The gardening tools are next to the tool / tall box.

Activity 3: Authentic Resource: Award Acceptance Speech

John Nash's 1994 Nobel Prize in Economic Sciences Acceptance Address from "A Beautiful Mind" (2002)

Thank you.

I've always believed in numbers and the equations and logics that lead to reason.

But after a lifetime of such pursuits, I ask, "What truly is logic?" "Who decides reason?" My quest has taken me through the physical, the metaphysical, the delusional – and back.

And I have made the most important discovery of my career, the most important discovery of my life: It is only in the mysterious equations of love that any logic or reasons can be found.

I'm only here tonight because of you [wife, Alicia]. You are the reason I am. You are all my reasons.

Thank you.

/ʊ/=underline

Review for Vowels

1. Read the following dialogue paying close attention to tense and lax vowels.

Jean	Hello, Pete. Come in. You look all flustered. Are you ok?
Pete	Sorry, I'm late. The traffic was really bad. But I picked up the things you asked for.
Jean	Oh, great! I hope it wasn't much trouble. Just put them on the table. Did you find everything?
Pete	No, they had black beans, ice cream, and rulers but not thumbtacks.
Jean	That's ok. I can get the tacks on my way to the pool on Saturday.
Pete	Other than the tacks, I think I got everything on the list, at least.
Jean	Well, thank you. Anyway, have a seat. Would you like some ice cream?
Pete	That'd be great. But before that, may I have something to drink?
Jean	Of course. How about peach or lemon iced tea? It's hot out, right?
Pete	Yes, it is! I need to cool off a bit. Peach sounds perfect.

*Record yourself and compare with the recorded sample.

2. Read the following dialogue paying close attention to reduced vowels.

Tricia	So are you going anywhere during the summer?
Kevin	I'm probably going on a family vacation to a log cabin in nearby mountain sometime in August.
Tricia	A log cabin? That sounds peaceful and refreshing. My family is planning to go to a beach. I wish we were going to the mountains.
Kevin	Why? What's wrong with the beach? The beach is always full of excitement and fun!
Tricia	Yea, exactly. You know, I prefer to relax and get plenty of sleep. I'm not exactly the hustle and bustle type.
Kevin	Oh, I love the beach. It's full of entertainment. Maybe you and I should swap our itineraries for this summer.

*Record yourself and compare with the recorded sample.

Answer key

3. Fill in the blanks with the words provided in the box and practice reading the passage aloud.

Most people dress neatly for work as an act of courtesy toward their employers and clients. But some people believe that dressing smartly will impress their bosses or customers to think they are more capable. When a person is judged according to their appearance, it is called lookism. In 2002, the American news show 20/20 investigated lookism by hiring good-looking actors and plain-looking actors to get help with buying a car, collecting money for charity, and applying for jobs. The better-looking actors were favored over the homey ones. Many think that this form of prejudice can be as serious as racism, sexism and age discrimination. But some also believe that certain businesses, especially services, need attractive employees to help draw customers.

*Record yourself and compare with the recorded sample.

4. Snow White and the Seven Dwarves

There once was a princess named Snow White who had an evil stepmother, the queen. Every day, the queen asked her magic mirror, "Mirror, mirror on the wall, who is the fairest one of all?" and the mirror always answered "you are." But one day, the mirror answered, "Snow White." The queen was very angry. She sent her servants to have Snow White killed. But the servants felt sorry for Snow White and let her go. Snow White wandered the forest, hungry and alone, until she came to a little cabin where the seven dwarves lived. She lived happily with the seven dwarves who let her live with them.

One day, the queen asked the mirror again, "Mirror, mirror on the wall, who is the fairest one of all?" and the mirror answered, "Snow White." The queen realized that Snow White was still alive. So the queen disguised herself as a peddler and gave Snow White a poisoned apple. Snow White took a bite and fell on the floor. The dwarves were very sad and put her in a glass coffin. Then, by chance, a prince came by and saw beautiful Snow White and bent down to give her a kiss. Snow White opened her eyes and woke up. They fell in love and lived happily ever after.

*Record yourself and compare with the recorded sample.

Unit 22 Letters, Numbers, Dates, Addresses

Acronyms

SOS	USC	BMW
GPS	MBA	CIA
IBM	PGA	CSI
IMF	ROK	DMB
JFK	USA	FBI

Emphasis=underline

Numbers-Teen vs. ty

thirteen	thirty
fourteen	forty
fifteen	fifty
sixteen	sixty
seventeen	seventy
eighteen	eighty
nineteen	ninety

Emphasis=underline

Activity 1

Hello. My name is Tae Kyung Yoon. The first name is two words, T-A-E and the second word is spelled K-Y-U-N-G. My last name is Y-O-O-N. I was born in September 27, 1985 in Seoul, and my major is economics. I'm very happy to meet you guys and you can reach me at tky01@email.com or 010-3546-6970. I'm looking forward to a great semester with you.

Name	Tae Kyung Yoon
Phone #	010-3546-6970
Email	tky01@email.com
Birthday	September 27, 1985

Unit 23 Descriptive & Set Phrases

Descriptive phrases	Set phrases
A white house	The **white** house
A light bulb	A **light** bulb
A gold fish	A **gold** fish
A dark room	A **dark** room
A hot dog	A **hot** dog
A green house	A **green** house

Stress=**bold**

Activity 1

Example	***English*** teacher
1	black **bird**
2	**white** house
3	**green** house
4	dark **room**
5	french **restaurant**
6	**hot** dog

Stress=**bold**

Activity 2

Waiter	Are you ready to order?
Customer	Yes, I'd like the cheeseburger combo.
Waiter	With that, you get French fries or onion rings.
Customer	I'll have the fries.
Waiter	And what would you like to drink?
Customer	Diet Coke, please.
Waiter	Will that be all?
Customer	Actually, do you have ice cream?
Waiter	Yes, we've got vanilla, chocolate, and strawberry ice cream.
Customer	I'll go with chocolate.

Set phrases=Underlined

Unit 24 Meaningless Utterances with Meanings

Activity 1

Jane	Excuse me, are you John?
John	Uh-huh.
Jane	Are you waiting for Mary?
John	Uh-huh.
Jane	Mary just asked me to tell you that she can't make it today.
John	Huh?
Jane	She got into a car accident.
John	Uh-uh!
Jane	It's a fender vender so it's not a big deal.
John	Oh.
Jane	But she says that she'll call when she gets out.
John	Uh-huh.

Utterances with meaning=underline

Activity 2

Jane	Hey, do you know what the homework was for today?
John	Hm, that's a good question. Did you do it?
Jane	Uh-uh. Did you?
John	Not yet. Let's see, what is the homework? Hm, it's...uh-oh.
Jane	Hmm? What?
John	It's a 10 page paper!
Jane	Uh-uh!! That's impossible! We wrote 10 pages last week!
John	Hmm, you're right. Can this be right or is it a typo?
Jane	Hmm, let me ask around.

Utterances with meaning=underline

Unit 25 Filler Utterances

Activity

John	Hey, Jane. How was the test? I mean, it was really hard.
Jane	Yea. It's like, really hard. We didn't learn these, did we?
John	Well, we did. But a long time ago, you know.
Jane	Yea! We covered it like in week 1 of the class!
John	I mean, I don't think anyone is going to get an A in this class.
Jane	Whatever! Don't worry about it, it's all good, you know.
John	Come on, How can you not worry about it? It's sort of important.
Jane	I mean, it's already over, man. You can't do anything about it.
John	Well, ok. I kind of see your point. What can you do?
Jane	Right. Come on. Let's just go study for the next exam.

Filler=Underline

Unit 26 Thought Groups

Activity 1

It was a warm sunny day in spring. I was coming home in the evening when someone said, "Help! Somebody help me!" I turned around to see what was going on. There was a lady sitting on the ground calling for help. I walked up to her and asked, "Is everything ok?" And she said, "No, I fell, and I can't get up." I figured she had sprained her ankle, so I helped her to a nearby bench, called the taxi, took her to the hospital, and I came home.

Activity 2

Yesterday, I woke up, ate breakfast, brushed my teeth and got ready to leave the house. Just when I was about to leave, the telephone rang, and of course, I picked up. There was nobody on the other line, so I hung up. Then it rang again. I said, "Hello? Who is this?" But no one answered. The same thing happened over and over, at least 10 times. I finally got fed up and called the police. In the evening, they told me that someone's baby was playing with the phone, and they told the parents to keep a better eye on their child.

General Patterns of Spoken English

Unit 27 Emphasis

Activity 1

John	Why didn't you call me last weekend?
Jane	I told you. I was working all weekend.
John	All weekend?

Emphasis=Underline

Activity 2

John	I can't remember where I put my phone at Mikey's.
Jane	You lost your phone and your keys?
John	No, I lost my phone at Mikey's!

Emphasis=Underline

Activity 3

Jane	Where are the supplies?
John	What surprise? Is it someone's birthday?
Jane	No. Supplies for the office.
John	Oh, office supplies. They're not here yet.

Emphasis=Underline

Activity 4

Jane	Call me at work if you need to. It's 354-5674
John	3-4-4-6-8-4?
Jane	No. 3-5-4 5-6-7-4
John	Oh, ok. I got it.

Emphasis=Underline

Unit 28 Added Details

Activity 1

John	I feel like a sandwich.
Jane	Me, too. Tuna sandwich sounds good.

Emphasis=Underline

Activity 2

Jane	May I have some coffee?
John	Sure.
Jane	Well, actually, coffee with cream, please.

Emphasis=Underline

Activity 3

Jane	Are you reading Milton's Paradise Lost?
John	Yea. Have you read it?
Jane	Yes, it's a very long.
John	I believe it's more than a thousand pages long.
Jane	Isn't it like thirteen hundred pages?
John	Yea, thirteen hundred and eighty three pages to be exact.

Emphasis=Underline

Unit 29 Contrasting and Showing Alternatives

Activity 1

Clerk	Are you paying with Visa or Mastercard?
Customer	Visa.
Clerk	Are you paying with Visa or Mastercard?
Customer	No, I'm paying with cash.

Emphasis=Underline

Activity 2

John	Do you prefer your steak rare or well-done?
Jane	Rare or well-done, it's just meat to me.

Emphasis=Underline

Activity 3

John	What's going on?
Jane	Not much. What are <u>you</u> up to?
John	I don't know. I was thinking that I need to get out.
Jane	Where are you going to go?
John	I don't know. I guess <u>shopping</u> or taking a <u>walk in the park</u> or..
Jane	Oh, <u>talking a walk</u> sounds good.
John	Do you want to come? How about the <u>park</u> or the <u>lake</u>?
Jane	Park <u>or</u> the lake, it doesn't matter. I just need some exercise.

Emphasis=<u>Underline</u>

Unit 30 Question Intonation

Activity 1

John	What <u>time</u> is it?
Jane	What time is it? It's time for you to be in <u>class</u>.
John	<u>Really?</u> Is it past <u>10</u>?
Jane	Its' already <u>10:30</u>! You're 30 minutes late.
John	Oh, no. I'm <u>late</u>? I've never been <u>late</u> before!

Emphasis=<u>Underline</u>

Activity 2

John	Hey, where is your <u>car</u>?
Jane	<u>Where's</u> my car? It's in the <u>parking</u> lot.
John	Are you <u>sure</u>? I thought you parked it there, too. But... <u>look</u>.
Jane	Oh <u>no</u>! <u>Where</u> is my <u>car</u>!

Emphasis=<u>Underline</u>

Unit 31 Tag Question Intonation

Activity 1

Mom	John, come and sit down for a second.
John	Yes, Mom. It's not going to be long, is it?
Mom	No. I told you to clean your room yesterday, didn't I?
John	Well, I was going to do it, but I had to run to the store and...
Mom	And you haven't taken the trash out, have you?
John	I'm sorry, but the trash is picked up tomorrow, isn't it?
Mom	Oh, you're right. It's tomorrow. Can you take it out in the morning?
John	Sure, and I'll clean my room tonight.

Tag questions=underline

Unit 32 Listening Well

Activity 1

John	I was walking home last night and it started to rain, just a little bit.
Jane	Uh-huh.
John	But I didn't have an umbrella so I just decided to run home really fast.
Jane	Oh.
John	And thought that if I run fast enough, I won't get too wet.
Jane	Yeah.
John	But then it started to pour, like there is no tomorrow.
Jane	Really.
John	By the time I got home, I was drenched and now I have a cold.
Jane	Oh, no.

Words and phrases used to show that you are listening=underline

Unit 33 Continuing a Story

Activity 1

Jane	Hey, John. Help me out.
John	What's the matter?
Jane	How do I get to the City Hall from here?
John	Oh, the City hall? Umm, you can take the subway or the bus.
Jane	Umm, I think I'd rather take the subway.
John	Ok. Let's see, if you get on the subway from here, it's line 3, so... umm... transfer to line 2 when you can.
Jane	Which stations are they?
John	Umm..I believe..er...just transfer to line 2 at the Seoul National University of Education. Yeah..and I think it'll take 30 minutes.
Jane	Alright. So get on the subway, transfer to line 2 at Seoul National University of Education, and er...it goes to the City hall?
John	Yes. Exactly.

Fillers used to continue a story=underline

Unit 34 Quoting Others

Activity 1

John	So are we all coming to the meeting on Wednesday at 8 a.m.?
Jane	No. Not Susan. She said that she might not be able to make it.
John	Really? She called me yesterday and said, "I'll see you on Wednesday."
Jane	I wonder why. This morning she was like, "I have to go to the airport."
John	She said to me that her mother is flying in at 7 p.m. That's probably why.
Jane	I see. She must have thought that the meeting was in the evening.
John	Wait a minute, maybe her mother is arriving in the morning.
Jane	Oh, I don't know. We should just call her ask her to be sure.
John	But she said, "don't call me unless it's an emergency!"
Jane	Oh, great. Let me send her a text message first.

Quoted speech=underline

Unit 35 Humor

Activity 1

Sarah	Hello.
Andy	Hi, Sarah, This is Andy.
Sarah	Hey, did you get to LA ok?
Andy	No. I'm actually stuck in Hawaii.
Sarah	What? What happened?
Andy	There was some weather problem so we landed in Honolulu.
Sarah	Oh, lucky you. Did the airline put you in a hotel?
Andy	Yeah, I'm staying at a five star hotel, but the weather is too nice.
Sarah	Oh, how terrible. That must be a real pain.
Andy	Hahaha, yeah. And the beach is only a block away.

Sarcastic expression=underline

General Patterns of Spoken English

Unit 36 Depending on the Context

Activity 1

Context 1	Role: friends who have not seen each other since elementary school Location: on college campus
John	Hey, What's up?
Jane	Oh, hi. How have you been?
John	Just fine. How about you?
Jane	Everything is all good.
John	Well, that's great.
John	Yeah, look, I'm sorry, but I have to go.
Jane	Sure, we'll catch up later. Take care.
John	Right. Give me a call, ok? Bye.

Emphasis=underline

Unit 37 Polite Alternatives

Activity 2

Suggested answer

John	What would you like?
Jane	It doesn't matter. I'll have whatever you're having.
John	Come on. What about milk?
Jane	Hmmm. That's ok. May I some Coke?
John	Pardon?
Jane	Coke, please.
Jane	Oh, Coke. Just a second.